op

cm

20—

THE MARBLE THRESHING FLOOR

Publications of the American Folklore Society
Memoir Series
General Editor, Wm. Hugh Jansen
Volume 57   1973

THE MARBLE
THRESHING FLOOR

A Collection of Greek Folksongs

By ELLEN FRYE

PUBLISHED FOR THE AMERICAN FOLKLORE SOCIETY BY
THE UNIVERSITY OF TEXAS PRESS: AUSTIN AND LONDON

Library of Congress Cataloging in Publication Data

Frye, Ellen, comp.
   The marble threshing floor.

   (Publications of the American Folklore Society.
Memoir series, v. 57)
   Unacc.; words in Greek and English.
   Bibliography: p.
   1. Folk-songs, Greek. I. Title. II. Series:
American Folklore Society, Memoirs, v. 57.
M1714.F79M3   784.4'06'09495   72-10975
ISBN 0-292-75005-6

CONTENTS

Epiros

Cyclades Islands

ILLUSTRATIONS

Following page 192

1. Yioryios Tsetsos, Singer from the Village of Metsovon, Epiros

2. Yioryios Tsetsos

3. Kostas Panorios, Singer and Violinist from the Village of Kardhiani, Island of Tinos

4. Ioannis Roudas, Sarakatsanos Singer from the Village of Vitsa in the Zaghori Region of Epiros

5. Wedding Dance in a Zaghori Village

6. Two Women, Village of Vitsa

7. Sarakatsanos Hut in a Zaghori Village

8. Wedding Procession in a Zaghori Village

PREFACE

This collection of 110 Greek folksongs is the result of an eighteen-month stay in Greece in 1963 and 1964 and a return trip in the summer of 1967. During the first period I spent about eight months reading and listening to tapes in the Folklore Archives of the Academy of Athens (now the Center of Research of Greek Folklore). Most of the spring, summer, and early-autumn months of 1964 I spent on the road with a Grundig TK 6 tape recorder; during that time I recorded over 300 songs in the Peloponnesos, Thessaly, Epiros, Macedonia, and a dozen of the islands. In July and August of 1967 I returned to Greece, this time with a Uher 4000L recorder, and taped another 64 songs on the islands of Tinos, Crete, and Rhodes and in the mountains of northern Epiros.

It is not a definitive or scholarly collection of Greek folk music. On both trips I was in Greece as a traveler; I used tape to record what was, to me, the most interesting aspect of Greek village life. However, many of the songs I collected have never been published before, and a surprising number were unknown to the scholars at the Folklore Archives. (Most of the tapes are deposited there as well as in the archives at Columbia University.)

I have been helped by many people in preparing this collection, and I would especially like to thank the following:

The singers who took time from their work to let me record their songs and whose names appear with the songs they sang; the many Greeks who took me into their homes and showed me the meaning of *filoxenia*, especially the Katsorides family in Athens, the Kazanas and Papakhatzis families in the village of Kato Panayia (Peloponnesos), the Erghas family on the island of Kalymnos, the Kozaris family in the village of Andigonia (Macedonia), and the Panorios family on the island of Tinos.

Also, George K. Spyridakis, former director of the Folklore Archives, for permitting me to study in the Archives and for making available its entire collection of tapes, books, and manuscripts, and also for unraveling several textual problems for me; Spyros Peristeris and Stavros Caracassis of the Folk Music Archives, and Costas D. Ioannides, Inspector of Music in Cyprus, who, along with Professor Spyridakis, guided my initial studies; and Ioannis Nikolaidis, secretary of the Institute for Epirotic Studies, for his assistance and hospitality on my Zaghori trip.

Also, Simon Karas of the Folk Music Department of the Greek National Radio and Stavros Caracassis, for checking and commenting on my material; Chrysoula Papadopoulou of Athens, for assisting me transcribe the lyrics; Mary Vouras, of Athens, for her invaluable comments on the notes and translations; and Ken Eisler, my husband, who accompanied me on the second trip and photographed the singers and musicians.

THE MARBLE THRESHING FLOOR

INTRODUCTION

Life in a Greek village is hard. The most common occupations—farming, herding, and fishing—require long hours and strong backs. Material rewards are scant. The endless struggle against the elements—rocky soil, sparse pastureland, storms, and droughts—is broken only by religious celebrations and seasonal festivals. But the Greek, instead of resigning himself to this harsh existence, throws himself into the *agon*, pitting himself and his family against the rest of the world. The battle itself, rather than the outcome, gives him his identity.[1]

While some Greek folksongs dwell on the pains and troubles of this life (particularly laments and emigration songs), many of them reflect this mood of embracing life; in so doing they draw strikingly vivid images from the struggle. A woman who has, since childhood, bundled the family clothes down a mountainside to wash them in a cold river and spread them to dry on the bank or available trees can still sing a love song that talks

[1] See Ernestine Friedl, *Vasilika: A Village in Modern Greece*, especially 75-76.

about washing clothes with tears and musk soap and drying them on the "bitter-almond tree that blooms in January" (*Song 20*).

Although the ubiquitous transistor radio has brought *bouzouki* and other popular music into the remotest regions, authentic folk singers can still be found in most villages and towns. Finding them is not difficult, although persistence and patience is often needed. In the smallest villages that I visited I usually asked the priest or village president; in larger villages and in towns I asked a coffeehouse owner or, more often, passersby on the street. Once the singers were found I asked them to sing all the local and regional songs they knew.

Many areas are fortunate enough to have folk instrumentalists who play for dances and weddings and occasional Sunday evenings in the coffeehouse. Their melody instruments—violin, clarinet, bagpipe—parallel the singer's voice, with embellishments, or answer it antiphonally, line by line. Between strophes the instrumentalists improvise passages using motifs from the song being accompanied and from other songs as well. These melody instruments are often accompanied by a guitar, or *laouto* (a four-stringed fretted instrument), playing open triads, or a drum or tambour beating out rhythmic *ostinati*, or by both.

Greeks cannot sing without their famous good mood, or *kefi*,[2] and on more than one occasion my request was refused because of a singer's personal troubles. Usually, however, setting up the tape recorder and a small audience produced the proper mood. An experience on the island of Skopelos is illustrative: A young girl whom I had recorded with her girl-friends told me that her father and aunt knew many good songs, and she invited me to her house. There her father assured me that he did indeed know many valuable songs but that he had worked in the fields all day and had no *kefi* for singing. He genuinely regretted the fact, especially since one of his songs, he said, was no longer known by anyone else on the island. I agreed that it was too bad and began recording his sister. We had taped only three songs when suddenly the opening lines of the special ballad burst out of the corner. His *kefi* had arrived.

One of the biggest advantages a collector has in Greece is the villagers' attitude toward their music. Songs were constantly being introduced to me as having great value, and onlookers often encouraged the singers by

---

[2] *Kefi* (good mood, gaiety, or gusto) implies a readiness to express the joy of living, either in buoyant conversation or in song.

reminding them that the songs would be going to Athens and to America where other people would have a chance to recognize their worth.

There are still some male singers who remember the great Byzantine epics of the Akritan oral cycle.[3] Commoner, however, are the more recent *kleftic*[4] ballads, historical songs chronicling the era before and during the Greek War for Independence (1821-1832) as well as later episodes in the development of the modern Greek state. These texts are sung to both dance tunes and "table" music;[5] some of them tell about battles and the deaths of heroes (e.g., *Song 30*), others simply describe *kleftic* life and attitudes (e.g., *Songs 2* and *3*).

One of the most important events in village life is the wedding, the public ceremony that marks the entry of a man and a woman into the adult world. The celebration often lasts several days, beginning with the laying out and inspection of the bride's dowry and going through the religious ceremony (always held on a Sunday) to the reception and dance that may last two or three days. Music is an essential part of the affair. Included in this collection are songs to accompany the inspection of the dowry (*Song 50*), the ceremonious shaving of the groom (*Song 81*), the wedding banquet (*Song 49*), and the newlyweds' leaving the church (*Song 51*), as well as several dance songs for the wedding reception (e.g., *Song 76*).

Religious holidays, like weddings, help break the monotony of the daily struggle. The most common type of religious folksong is the *kalanda*, or carol, which is sung from house to house on Christmas, New Year's, Epiphany, the Day of Lazarus, and Palm Sunday. The singers are often small boys who accompany themselves with triangles and drums and are rewarded with *koulouria* (small ring-shaped biscuits), fruit and nuts, or small coins.

---

[3] See James A. Notopoulos, *Modern Greek Heroic Oral Poetry*. *Song 78* is a fragment from this cycle and is today sung as a wedding song.

[4] *Klefts* (literally "thieves" or "brigands") were mountain guerrillas who combined a life of plundering with resistance to the Turkish Occupation. At times they cooperated with the enemy and took on the duties of a militia (called *armatoli*, or "armed men"). They were often a terror to Greek and Turkish villagers alike, but, because of their heroic way of life and their decisive part in winning the Greek War for Independence, they have become the heroes of modern Greece. For a description of *kleftic* life see John W. Baggally, *Greek Historical Folksongs*, 1-26.

[5] "Table" songs (τραγούδια τῆς τάβλας) are solo songs that are usually sung around a table—full of coffee cups or ouzo glasses in a coffeehouse or heaped with banquet food at a celebration. They are rhythmically free, highly ornamented melodies sung in a melismatic style. (See *Song 3*.)

The *kalanda* often open with a one- or two-line formula bidding good
evening to the "nobles" of the house or perhaps assuring the family that
the singers did not come just for the reward (see *Song 92*). They continue
with a narrative related—however obliquely—to the event being celebrated:
Christ's birth, the death and resurrection of Lazarus, and so on.

Following the narrative, especially of the Christmas and New Year's
kalanda, are "praises" (*penemata*) for the various members of the family.
The master, for example, deserves a great ship to sail in (*Song 108*), or the
daughter is going to need a large dowry because such an important person
is asking for her hand (*Song 92*).

Kalanda usually end with a few lines asking for a reward (*Song 66*) and a
spoken or chanted formula wishing good luck for the new year.[6]

The folk view of Greek Orthodoxy is a mixture of Biblical and historical
fact seasoned with folklore and a good deal of paganism left over from
ancient Greek practice.[7] In the religious folksongs the emphasis is often on
the human traits of the holy personages. The Virgin Mary is seen as a real
woman and mother. In one Christmas *kalanda* she lies in labor and says,

> Help me, I pray
> in this blessed hour,
> this glorious hour
> and go fetch the midwife.[8]

And in her Easter lament (*Song 13*) she asks Saint John for news of her
son and then faints when she learns of his death.

New Year's Day is dedicated to Saint Vasili (Basil), the fourth-century
bishop from Caesaria (now called Kayseri) in the province of Cappodocia
in Asia Minor. In the most common New Year's *kalanda* he is a young
scholar on his way to school. He is stopped (sometimes by three angels)
and asked to recite the alphabet. Before he can begin, a miracle takes
place: his walking stick is transformed into a tree from which partridges
fly down and wash their wings and sprinkle the master of the house where
the *kalanda* is being sung (*Song 108*).

---

[6] Although these different formulae are written out at the end of each *kalanda*, I
have not translated any of them, because they are so compressed. The most common
one is "*καί τοῦ χρόνου*," literally, "and of next year"; the wish is, roughly, "may all
the days of the coming year be successful."

[7] See J.C. Lawson, *Modern Greek Folklore and Ancient Greek Religion*.

[8] From G.A. Megas, *Greek Calendar Customs*, 28.

In a less well known *kalanda*, especially popular where farming is the main profession, Vasili is out ploughing his fields. He meets Christ; they exchange greetings and talk shop ("How many bushels have you planted?"); and Christ blesses the ploughing team. The miracle in this *kalanda* is like the miracle of the loaves and fishes (Matt. 6:41 - 44): birds and rabbits eat all the grain, but the leftovers still measure in the thousands. A tree springs up where Christ was standing, and again partridges wash their wings and sprinkle the master.[9]

Another type of song I frequently encountered was the emigration song or "song of the foreign land" (τραγοῦδι τῆς ξενητειᾶς). Such songs developed out of the long-standing Greek tradition of sending sons and husbands off to work in more prosperous countries to supplement the family income. Traditionally these foreign lands were other parts of the Ottoman Empire, such as Constantinople or Alexandria. Now, all too often they are Australia, New Zealand, or North America, where distance makes the emigration semipermanent. With family ties as close as they are in Greece, leaving home for any length of time is unbearable, for both the emigrant and the family he leaves behind; the emigration songs express eloquently this pain of separation (*Song 1*).

In addition to *kleftic*, wedding, religious, and emigration songs, I have included in this collection ballads or ballad fragments (e.g., *Song 61*); *mandinadhes* (extemporized rhymed distiches in the fifteen-syllable political meter, e.g., *Song 69*); songs for non-religious holidays, such as Carnival (*Song 52*), March 1st (*Song 46*), or Mayday (*Song 54*); a grape-harvesting song (*Song 89*); a lullaby (*Song 90*); an election song (*Song 93*); a lament for a national statesman (*Song 12*); and many dance songs.[10]

The music of the songs[11] is as varied as the texts. All the diatonic modes are found in Greek folk music; this collection includes melodies in the following complete diatonic modes:

---

[9] *Songs 43, 92*, and *110* all contain elements of this farmer's *kalanda*. A Cretan variant that is slightly less confused is in G.A. Megas, Ἑλληνικαί ἑορταί καί ἔθιμα τῆς λαικῆς λατρείας, 63-64.

[10] I have identified the dance songs only when my informants so named them. Descriptions of the different dances are in Ricky Holden and Mary Vouras, *Greek Folk Dances*.

[11] To Greek singers, the song (τό τραγοῦδι) is the text; the music is referred to as ὁ σκοπός.

la mode (e.g., *Song 44*)
do mode (e.g., *Song 67*)
re mode (e.g., *Song 32*)
mi mode (e.g., *Song 94*)
ti mode (*Song 72*)
fa mode (*Song 108*)[12]

The most common diatonic mode, the *re* mode, is found, in addition to its pure form, in several different shadings created by raising or lowering one of the intermediate notes (e.g., *Song 27*).

The majority of the melodies in this collection have a range of only four, five, or six notes and thus use only the first tetra-, penta-, or hexachord of the diatonic modes. For example, *Song 16* uses a *re* tetrachord (with one subtonic note); *Song 61* uses a *mi* pentachord; and *Song 38* uses a *do* tetrachord.

The most common chromatic scale found in Greek music consists of two chromatic tetrachords connected disjunctly by a whole tone, as in the example below.

There is no example of this complete scale in the present collection, although there are many melodies that use its first tetra-, penta-, or hexachord (e.g., *Song 18*).

Gapped modes, although uncommon, are occasionally found in Epiros. *Song 24* uses the *la* pentaton, and *Song 25* uses a *mi* hexaton (sixth degree missing).

Mixed modes are formed by combining a chromatic tetrachord with a diatonic one, either conjunctly or disjunctly. The most common mixed mode consists of a chromatic tetrachord combined conjunctly with a *re* tetra- or pentachord (as in *Song 1*).[13]

---

[12] This song, however, lacks the upper fourth degree of the mode, thus leaving the melody without the tri-tone characteristic of the *fa* mode. Moreover, due to the cyclical nature of the song, the *fa* tonic is not evident to the ear until the final note.

[13] Eight other mixed modes found in Greek and Cypriot music are listed in C.D. Ioannides, Φωνητικά γυμνάσματα καί παιδαγωγικά τραγούδια, 141-142.

Some Greek melodies use two alternating modes, usually with a common tonic but occasionally with different tonics. *Song 107* uses a chromatic hexachord in section A and a *re* pentachord in section B, with *re* as the common tonic. *Song 31* begins with a *re* tetrachord and at the end of the second bar of section B changes to a chromatic tetrachord with a tonic *do*. *Song 77* is in the *ti* mode throughout section A, but in section B the fifth degree is unstable, and the melody alternates between the *ti* mode and the *mi* mode.

Rhythmically the songs fall into three categories: (1) those which are completely free (i.e., having no meter and no fixed unit of stress), such as *Song 3*; (2) those which are measured (i.e., having no meter and no regular phrases, but a fixed unit of stress), such as *Song 50*; and (3) metered songs. Metered songs use, in addition to the universal duple and triple meters of 2/4, 3/4, and 4/4, many additive meters. Included in this collection are:

$$5/8 = \frac{2+3}{8} \ (Song \ 57)$$

$$6/4 = \frac{(2+1)+(1+2)}{4} \ \text{or} \ \frac{(1+2)+(2+1)}{4} \ (\text{e.g.,} \ Songs \ 2 \ and \ 15, \text{respectively})[14]$$

$$7/8 = \frac{3+2+2}{8} \ (\text{e.g.,} \ Song \ 59)$$

$$7/4 = \frac{3+2+2}{4} \ (Song \ 84)$$

$$11/8 = \frac{(2+3)+(2+2+2)}{8} \ (Song \ 41)$$

Some songs have two meters, usually with the A section in one and the

---

[14] For a discussion of the 6/4 meter see Spyros Peristeris, 'O 'εξάσημος ρυθμός εἰς τά 'Ελληνικά δημοτικά τραγούδια.

B in another (as *Song 46*);[15] other songs begin irregularly and then move into a meter (as *Song 75*).[16]

The musical transcriptions in this work are of one musical strophe only, usually the first. Since the melodies often vary a great deal from strophe to strophe, from performance to performance, and, of course, from singer to singer, the transcriptions should not be thought of as representations of songs, but rather as extracts from performances. As such, they do not reflect either the versatility of the singer—his ability to vary endlessly a basic tune—or the variability of the song itself.

The song texts consist of two elements: (1) the lyrics, in which are represented many different poetic meters (about two-thirds of those presented here are in the fifteen-syllable iambic rhymed or unrhymed); and (2) metrically extraneous words and phrases (called *tsakismata*), which, along with part-line repetitions, are used to fill out the poetic line to fit the musical line.

In most of the texts, the repetitions and *tsakismata* follow a set pattern for each musical strophe. In these cases, the complete texts, with *tsakismata* and repetitions underlined, are transcribed for only the first or the first and second musical strophes. (In the texts set to the music, however, the *tsakismata*, but not the repetitions, are underlined.) Songs in which the pattern changes or is ambiguous are written out completely.

The line count to the left of the text applies to the metric line, not to the complete text.

The translations are as literal as I could make them. They follow the Greek text line by line, except that all the repetitions and *tsakismata* are omitted, along with *yirismata* (distiches that are added between strophes or at the end of the song), unless these are relevant to the rest of the song. The line count to the left of the translations coincides with the line count of the Greek text.

I have made no attempt to reproduce the poetic meters and rhyme

---

[15] These dual-metered songs are sometimes "mixed" dances; i.e., dances to which two different sets of steps are danced. See Sotirios Chianis, "Some Observations on the Mixed-Dance in the Peloponnesus," Λαογραφία (1959): 244-256.

[16] The preceding discussion of the musical characteristics of Greek folksong is limited to observations about my own fairly small collection. For broader descriptions in English see G.A. Megas and Spyros Peristeris, *Folk Music of Greece*, 6; G.K. Spyridakis and Spyros Peristeris, Ἑλληνικά δημοτικά τραγούδια: μουσική ἐκλογή, 422-430; and Solon Michaelides, *The Neohellenic Folk-Music*, 9-22.

schemes of the Greek lyrics. However, where the lyrics are rhymed couplets or quatrains, these are separated into strophes.

Words that were not easily translatable I have left in the original Greek; they are explained in the glossary.

SYMBOLS USED IN
THE TRANSCRIPTIONS

  ↑   Pitch slightly higher than written
  ↓   Pitch slightly lower than written
  ~   Vibrato
  ↗   Slow portamento
  ╱   Fast portamento
  ×ˡ Note of uncertain pitch
  ∩   Duration slightly longer than written
  ∪   Duration slightly shorter than written
  ⌒— Group of notes, all slightly longer than written
  ⌣— Group of notes, all slightly shorter than written
  ʔ   Breath mark, usually consisting of one or two beats
  ⊡   Strophe 1
  〔1〕 Line 1

THE SONGS (BY REGION)

Η ΠΕΛΟΠΟΝΝΗΣΟΣ

THE PELOPONNESOS

1. Ο ΑΜΑΡΑΝΤΟΣ (Τῆς ξενητειᾶς)

Κωνσταντῖνος Μπρούτζας
Τρίπολις, ᾿Αρκαδίας

᾿Ὤχ, γιά ἰδέ-, καλέ, γιά ἰδέ-, γιά ἰδέστε τόν ἀϊμάραντο,
γιά ἰδέστε τόν ἀϊμάραντο· σέ τί βουνά φυτρώνει, καλέ;

Φυτρώνει μέσ᾿ στά δίστρατα, στίς πέτρες, στά λιθάρια.
᾿Όποιος τόν κόψει, κόβεται κι ὅποιος τόν φά᾿ πεθαίνει.
Δέν τὄτρωγε καί ἡ μάνα μου πρωτοῦ εἶχει κάνει ἐμένα.
5 Κι ἄν μ᾿ ἔκανε, τί μ᾿ ἔθελε κι ἄν μ᾿ ἔχει, τί μέ θέλει;

Πού 'γώ στά ξένα περπατώ, στά ξένα τρώω καί πίνω·
ξένοι μοῦ πλένουν τά σκουτιά, ξένοι τά σιδερώνουν.

THE AMARANTH (Emigration song)

Look at the amaranth—what mountain does it bloom on?
It blooms at the fork of the road, on the stones, on the rocks.
Whoever cuts it, cuts himself; whoever eats it, dies.
Why didn't my mother eat it before she bore me?
5 If she bore me, why did she want me; if she has me, what
        does she want me for?
I who walk in foreign lands, who eat and drink in foreign lands,
and foreigners wash and iron my clothes.

2. ΠΕΡΔΙΚΟΥΛΑ ΤΟΥ ΜΩΡΕΑ (Τσάμικος χορός)

'Αργύριος Σταυρόπουλος
Χ. Βυτίνα, 'Αρκαδίας

— Ωρέ, μωρ' περδικούλα, ἄχ, μωρ' περδικούλα τοῦ Μωρηά,
μωρ' περδικούλα τοῦ Μωρηά κοσμοπερπατημένη,

Ν-ἐφτοῦ ψηλά πού πέτεσαι καί χαμηλ' ἀγνατεύεις,
μήν εἶδες κλέφτες πουθενά, τούς Κολοκοτρωναίους;
—Ν-ἐψές προψές τούς εἴδαμε ψηλά στά Κανελάκια
5   καί στοῦ Τσαλτῆ τόν ἔλατο καί στή γραμμένη πλάκα.
Ν-εἶχαν ἀρνιά καί ψένανε καί κριάρια καί σουβλίζαν·
ν-εἶχαν κ'ἕνα καλό κρασί ν-ἀπ' τούς Ἁγιωθοδώρους·
ν-εἴχανε καί τό δήμαρχο, δήμαρχο τῆς Βυτίνας.

LITTLE PARTRIDGE OF MOREA (*Tsamikos* dance)

"Little partridge of Morea, world traveler,
there high up where you're flying you can survey below you.
Did you happen to see the *klefts* anywhere, the Kolokotronis band?"
"Yesterday and the day before we saw them, high up on Kanelakia
5   and at Tsaldi's pine tree and plaque.
They had sheep roasting and rams on the spit
and good wine from the Ayiothodhorous family,
and they had with them the mayor of Vytina."

3. ΟΙ ΚΟΛΟΚΟΤΡΩΝΑΙΟΙ (Τῆς τάβλας)

Ἀργύριος Σταυρόπουλος
Χ. Βυτίνα, Ἀρκαδίας

Λά - μπει ν-δ _____

ἤ-, _____ μω - ρέ ν-δ ἤ - - -

λιος ____ στά ____ βου - - ου - - - -

νά ____ Λά- μπει καί στά ____ λα - -

γκά-δια ____ Λά - μπει καί _____

στ᾽ ᾽Α-, _____ μω - ρέ, καί στ᾽ ᾽Αρ - κου-

δό - - ρε - - - - μα _____ .

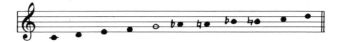

Λάμπει ν-ὸ ἥ-, μωρέ, ν-ὸ ἥλιος στά βουνά, λάμπει καί στά λαγκάδια,
λάμπει καί στ᾽ Ἀ-, μωρέ, καί στ᾽ Ἀρκουδόρεμα,

λάμπει καί στ᾽ Ἀ-, μωρέ, καί στ᾽ ᾽ Ἀρκουδόρεμα, στά δάλιο Λιμποβίσι.
Πό ᾽κεῖ ᾽ναι οἱ κλέ-, μωρέ, οἱ κλέφτες οἱ πολλοί,

Πό ᾽κεῖ ᾽ναι οἱ κλέφτες οἱ πολλοί, οἱ Κολοκοτρωναῖοι.
Μ᾽ αὐτοί δέν καταδέχονται τή γῆ νά τή πατήσουν:
5   καβάλλα πᾶνε στήν ἐκκλησιά, καβάλλα προσκυνᾶνε,
καβάλλα παίρνουν ἀντίδερο.

THE KOLOKOTRONIS BAND OF *KLEFTS* (Table song)

The sun shines on the mountains and in the valleys,
it shines on Arkoudhorema, on torchlike Limbovisi.
All the *klefts* are [gathered] there, the Kolokotronis band.
But they don't condescend to tread on the ground:
5   on horseback they go to church; on horseback they worship;
on horseback they take the holy bread.

4. ΣΙΓΑΛΑ ΒΡΕΧΕΙ Ο ΟΥΡΑΝΟΣ (Καλαματιανός)

Γρηγόριος Σταυρόπουλος, Βασίλειος Σταυρόπουλος, καί Χρυσόστομος Σταυρόπουλος
Χ. Βυτίνα, 'Αρκαδίας

Σι - γα - λά,   βρ'ἀ-μάν   ἀ - μάν,

Σι - γα - λά βρέχ' οὐ - ρα - νός   Σι - γα - λά βρέχ'

οὐ - ρα - νός   Σι - γα - λός ψι - χα - λισ - μός.

Σιγαλά, βρ᾿ ἀμάν ἀμάν, σιγαλά βρέχ᾿ οὐρανός,
σιγαλά βρέχ᾿ οὐρανός, σιγαλός ψιχαλισμός.

Σιγαλά πάω κ᾿ ἐγώ
στήν ἀγάπη ὅπ᾿ ἀγαπῶ.

5   Θά τή βρίσκω μαλωμένη
καί βαρειά βαλαντωμένη.

—Τί ἔχεις, κόρη μου, καί κλαῖς;
Κ᾿ ἐμένανε δέ μοῦ τό λές;

Μή σέ μάλωσε κανείς;
10 Κόρη μου, νά μοῦ τό εἰπῆς.

—Μέ μαλώνει ἡ μάνα μου
καί μ' ἔδειρ'ό πατέρας μου.

Μέ μαλώνει κι ἀδελφός μου,
τά ματάκια καί τό φῶς μου.

SOFTLY THE RAIN FALLS (*Kalamatianos* dance)

Softly the rain falls,
a soft drizzle,

and softly I'm going
to my love.

5 I find her chastened
and exhausted.

"What's wrong, *kori*?
Tell me why you're crying.

Did someone scold you?
10 Tell me, *kori*."

"My mother scolded me
and my father beat me

and my brother scolded me, too,
my dearest brother."

5. ΚΑΛΑΝΤΑ ΤΩΝ ΦΩΤΩΝ

Εὐαγγελία Παντελία
Καλαμάτα, Μεσσηνίας

[2] Μέ χα - ρά με - γά - λη στούς ἄρ - χόν - τες.

Ἦρθανε τά φῶτα καί οἱ φωτεινές
μέ χαρά μεγάλη στούς ἄρχοντες.
Περπατεῖ ἡ κυρά μας στή γῆ, στή γῆ·
σπάργανα μαζεύει, κερί κρατεῖ.
5 Τόν ἀφέντη ᾽Άη Γιάννη περικαλεῖ:
—᾽Αφέντη, ἀφέντη ᾽Άη Γιάννη καί Βαπτιστῆ,
δύνοσαι νά Βαφτίσης θεοῦ παιδί;
—Δύνομεν καί θέλω καί περικαλῶ
ν᾽ ἀνεβῶ στούς ἀγιούς καί στούς οὐρανούς,
10 Νά μαζέψω μόσχο καί λιβανό.

Ν᾽ ἀγιαστοῦνε οἱ βρύσες καί τά νερά,
ν᾽ ἀγιαστῆ κι ἀφέντης μέ τήν κυρά.
᾽Έτη πολλά.

KALANDA FOR EPIPHANY

Epiphany has come
with great joy for the nobles.

Our Lady walks on earth,
gathering up swaddling clothes, holding a candle.
5   She begs *afendi* Saint John:
"*Afendi* Saint John the Baptist,
are you able to baptize God's Child?"
"I am able and willing, and I pray
that I may go up to the saints and the heavens
10   and gather up musk and incense."

May the springs and the waters become holy,
may our *afendi* and his lady become holy.

6. ΜΑΖΕΥ΄ ΤΑ ΠΕΡΙΣΤΕΡΙΑ ΣΟΥ, ΚΥΡΑ ΜΟΥ

Γεώργιος Δούκας
Χ. Ξηροκάμπι, Λακωνίας

'Ωρέ, μάζευ' τά πε-, μάζευ' τά περιστέρια σου, κυρά μου,
γιατ' έρχονται στήν αὐλή μου, Πατροκαλαματιανή μου.

'Ωρέ, μοῦ τρῶνε τό, μοῦ τρῶνε τό σιτάρι μου, κυρά μου,
καί μοῦ πίνουν τό νερό μου, Πατροκαλαματιανό μου.

5   'Ωρέ, βάζουνε καί, βάζουνε καί στά νύχια τους, κυρά μου,
ὤχ, τά χῶμα τῆς αὐλῆς μου, Πατροκαλαματιανή μου.

ROUND UP YOUR PIGEONS, LADY

Round up your pigeons, lady,
because they're coming into my courtyard.
They're eating up my wheat
and drinking up my water
5 and scratching up
the earth in my courtyard.

7. Η ΚΛΩΣΣΑ

'Αγγελία Φοτάκι
Χ. Κάτω Παναγία, 'Ηλείας

Κλῶσ-σα, τά που - λιά, κλῶσ-σα τά που - λιά

Κλῶσ-σα, τά που - λιά, δέν τἄ - βγα - λες σω - στά.

Σοῦ - βα - λα, σοῦ - βα - λα εἴ - κο - σι ἔ - να,

Μά δέν___ μοῦ-, μά δέν μοῦ-βγα - λες κα - νέ - να.

Κλῶσσα, τά πουλιά, (τρίς)
δέν τἄβγαλες σωστά.
Σούβαλα, σούβαλα εἴκοσι-ἔνα,
μά δέν μοῦ-, μά δέν μοῦβγαλες κανένα.

5 Κότα κλώσσισε
κ' ὕστερα ψόφισε.
'Άχ, διαβολουκόρη κλῶσσα,
φέτος θά σέ κάνω γρόσσα.

Μά ἴνας πετεινός
10 κόκκινος παρδαλός
μᾶς ἐτσίμπισε τήν κότα
στῆς γειτόνισσας τήν πόρτα.

THE BROODY HEN

Broody hen, the chicks,
you didn't hatch them right.
I set twenty-one eggs under you,
but you didn't hatch me any [of them].

5 Hatch your eggs, hen,
and afterward you can die.
Ah, you devil's daughter,
I'm going to make money on you this year!

A rooster,
10 red and spotted,
pecked our hen
in front of the neighbor lady's door.

8. ΚΟΚΚΙΝΑ ΜΑΝΤΕΡΙΝΑΚΙΑ (Συρτός πολίτικος)

Νίκη Δουβίτσα
Χ. Κάτω Παναγία, Ἠλείας

Κόκ - κι - να___ μαν - τε - ρι - νά - κια___

φύλ - λα___ πρα - σι - να,___ ἀ - μάν ἀ - μάν·

Εἰς ὑ - γεί - α___ στήν πα - - ρέ - α___

κ'ἔ - - ξω βα - - σα - να.

Κόκκινα μαντερινάκια, φύλλα πράσινα, ἀμάν ἀμάν·
εἰς ὑγεία στήν παρέα κ᾽ ἔξω βάσανα.

᾽Όλο οὖζο, ὅλο οὖζο, τό βαρέθηκα, ἀμάν ἀμάν·
δῶστε μου κ᾽ ἕνα κρασάκι πού τ᾽ ὀρέχτηκα.

5 Σάλα, σάλα, μέσ᾽ στή σάλα τά μιλήσαμε, ἀμάν ἀμάν,
νά σέ πάρω, νά μέ πάρης, συμφωνήσαμε.

LITTLE RED TANGERINES (*Syrtos politikos* dance)

Little red tangerines, green leaves—
a toast to companions and be done with troubles.

Ouzo, always ouzo, I'm tired of it,
give me the little glass of wine that I'm longing for.

5   We talked it over in the parlor,
and we agreed to marry.

9. ΜΠΑΛΛΟΣ

' Αγγελία Φοτάκι
Χ. Κάτω Παναγία, Ήλείας

Ή - βγα-νε πά - λι στό___ χο - - ρό, Ή -

βγα-νε πά - λι στό___ χο - - ρο, Ή -

βγα - νε πά - λι στό___ χο - - -

ρό Συρ-τό γιά___ νά χο - ρέ - - - ψουν.

Γύρισμα

Σάν πᾶς στά ξέ - να___ πά -

ρε κ'έ - μέ - να, Πά -

ρε___ κ'έ - μέ - - να___ γιά

μἔ - χεις συν - - τρο - φιά.

Γύρισμα:
Λά λά λά κτλ.

' Ἤβγανε πάλι στό χορό (τρίς)
συρτό γιά νά χορέψουν.

Γύρισμα:
Λά λά λά κτλ.

Τραγούδια καί πενέματα, (τρίς)
πολλά θά μᾶς γυρέψουν.

Γύρισμα:
Σάν πᾶς στά ξένα
Πάρε κ' ἐμένα,
5   Πάρε κ' ἐμένα νά μ' ἔχεις συντροφιά.
Λά λά λά κτλ.

Μαυροματοῦ, μαυροφρυδοῦ, μαῦρα καί τά μαλλιά σου,
Χωρίς νά θέλει ὁ ἄνθρωπος πέφτει στόν ἔρωτά σου.

BALLOS DANCE

They've started the dance again, to dance a *syrtos*.
They'll find many songs and praise—rhymes just for us.

Yirisma:

As you go away to the foreign land,
take me with you,
5   take me with you for company.

Black eyes, black eyebrows, black hair—
without wanting to, man falls in love with you.

10. ΚΡΗΤΙΚΙΑ ΜΟΥ ΛΕΜΟΝΙΑ

'Αγγελία Φοτάκι καί Νίκη Δουβίτσα
Χ. Κάτω Παναγία, ' Ηλείας

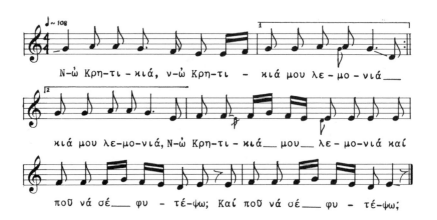

N-ὠ Κρητικιά, ν–ὠ Κρητικιά μου λεμονιά,
ν-ὠ Κρητικιά μου λεμονιά καί ποῦ νά σέ φυτέψω;
καί ποῦ νά σέ φυτέψω;

Νά σέ φυτέψω στό βουνό, φοβοῦμ' νά μή σέ κλέψουν.
Νά σέ φυτέψω στήν καρδιάν, ἴσως καί σέ κερδέσω.

N-ὁ κρητικός κι ἄς στολιστῆ καί βάλει τά καλά του.
5   ' ' Ολοι τόνε ζηλεύωνε ἀπ' τήν περπατηξιά του.

Στήν Κρήτην ἔχει ἔμορφες καί στά Χανιά γεμάτες
καί μέσα στόν ' Ηράκλειο ξανθές καί μαυρομάτες.

Πότε τσέ πότε τσέ πότε, πότε θά παντρευθούμε;
Πότε οἱ ἀδελφούλες σου "νυφούλα" θά μέ ποῦνε;

10   Στή Σούδαν ἐπληγώθηκα καί στά Χανιά θά γιάνω·
καί μέσα στόν ῾Ηράκλειο θά πέσω ν᾽ ἀποθάνω.

MY CRETAN LEMON TREE

Oh, my Cretan lemon tree, where shall I plant you?
If I plant you on the mountain, I'm afraid they'll steal you.
Let me plant you in my heart; perhaps I'll win you.

Let the Cretan get dressed and put on his best clothes.
5   Everyone is jealous of his fine bearing.

In Crete there are beautiful girls, and in Khania plump ones,
and in Iraklion blondes with black eyes.

When, oh when, oh when, when are we getting married?
When will your sisters call me "sister-in-law"?

10   At Soudha I was wounded, and in Khania I'll be cured,
and in Iraklion I'll fall down and die.

11. ΜΗ ΜΕ ΣΤΕΛΝΗΣ, ΜΑΝΑ, ΣΤΗΝ ΑΜΕΡΙΚΗ
(Τῆς ξενιτειᾶς)

'Αργυρώ 'Αραβαντίνου
Χ. Κάτω Παναγία, ' Ηλείας

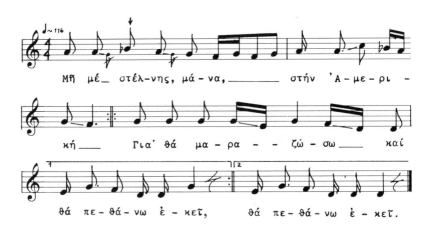

Μῆ μέ στέλ-νης, μά - να,＿＿＿＿ στήν 'Α - με - ρι - κή ＿ Για' θά μα - ρα - - ζώ - σω ＿ καί θά πε - θά - νω ἐ - κεῖ, θά πε - θά - νω ἐ - κεῖ.

Μῆ μέ στέλνης, μάνα, στήν 'Αμερική
για' θά μαραζώσω καί θά πεθάνω ἐκεῖ.

Δολλάρια δέν θέλω, πῶς θέλεις νά στὄ εἰπῶ;
Καλιό ψωμί, κρεμμύδι κ' ἐκεῖνον π' ἀγαπῶ.

5   'Αγαπῶ, μανούλα μ', κάποιο στό χωριό:
ἔμορφο λεβέντη καί μονάχο γυιό.

Μ'ἔχει φιλημένη μέσ' στίς ρεματιές
καί ἀγκαλιασμένη κάτ' ἀπ' τίς ἰτιές.

Φεύγω, Γιῶργιο μ᾽, φεύγω, πάω μακρυά,
10 πά᾽ νά μέ παντρέψουν μέσ᾽ στήν ξενιθειά.

Σάν ἀρνί μέ πᾶνε νά μέ σφάξουνε
καί ἀπ᾽ τόν καϋμό μου θά μέ θάψουνε.

MOTHER, PLEASE DON'T SEND ME TO AMERICA
(Emigration song)

Mother, please don't send me to America,
because I'll wither and die there.

I don't want any dollars, how can I tell you this—
only good bread, onions, and the man I love.

5 Little mother, I love someone in the village,
a handsome *levendi*, an only son.

He's kissed me in the ravines
and embraced me underneath the willows.

I'm leaving, Yioryio, I'm going far away,
10 I'm going to be married off in a foreign country.

Like a sheep they're taking me to the slaughter,
and from my sorrow they'll bury me.

12. ΜΟΙΡΟΛΟΓΙ ΠΡΟΣ ΤΟΝ ΒΕΝΙΖΕΛΟΝ

Γαρυφαλιά Σουρή
Χ. Κάτω Παναγία, ʾ Ηλείας

Τί ἦ-ταν αὐ - τό____ πού πά - θα - - με;

τί μαύρ' αὐ - τό____ χα - μπέ - - - ρι;

Τόν Βε - νι - ζέ - λο____ ἐ - χά - σα - με, ἄχ, ____

τόν λα-τρευ-τό____ ʾ Λευ-τέ - - ρι ____

Τόν Βε - νι - ζέ - λο____ ἐ - χά - σα - με, ἄχ, ____

τόν λα - τρευ-τό____ ʾ Λευ - τέ - - - ρι.

Τί ἦταν αὐτό πού πάθαμε; τί μαῦρ' αὐτό χαμπέρι;
Τόν Βενιζέλο ἐχάσαμι, ἄχ, τόν λατρευτό 'Λευτέρη. (δίς)

'Λευτέρη μας, πατέρα μας, τῆς Κρήτης τό καμάρι,
τόν χωρισμόν σου ποιός μπορεῖ μέ ὑπομονή νά πάρη; (δίς)

5 Μᾶς τίμησες, μᾶς δόξασες, ἐμᾶς καί τήν πατρίδα,
τήν 'λευτεριά μᾶς ἔδωσες κ' ἤσουν γιά μᾶς ἐλπίδα. (δίς)

Κρήτη μου, ἔχεις ὀμορφιές ὅπου δέν ἔχεις ταίρι·
' ἔχεις καί κάτι ζηλευτό: τόν τάφο τοῦ 'Λευτέρη.

LAMENT FOR VENIZELOS

What is this that has happened; what black news is this?
We've lost our Venizelos, our adored 'Lefteri.

'Lefteri, our father, pride of Crete,
who can bear your departure?

5 You honored us, you brought us glory, us and the homeland;
you gave us freedom and you were our hope.

Crete, you've got beautiful girls, girls without peer,
and you've got something else to be envied: the tomb of 'Lefteri.

13. ΜΟΙΡΟΛΟΓΙ ΤΗΣ ΠΑΝΑΓΙΑΣ

Καλιόπη Ζαργανᾶ, Μαρία Μινιότη, Ντίνα
Μανιάτη, ᾿Αθανᾶ Καμένου, καί ᾿Αγγελία
Φοτάκι
Χ. Κάτω Παναγία, ᾿Ηλείας

Τώ - ρα, _____ τώ - ρα 'ν' ἁ - γία _____

Σα - - - ρα - κο - στή, Τώ - ρα 'ν' ἁ -

γίες _____ ἡ - - - - - μέ - ρες

Τώρα, τώρα 'ν' ἁγία Σαρακοστή, τώρα 'ν' ἁγίες ἡμέρες

Πού λειτουργοῦν οἱ ἐκκλησιές καί ψέλνουν οἱ παπάδες.
Καί, μέ τό κύριε ἐλέησο καί τίς τιμιωτέρες,
τό μοιρολόϊ τοῦ Χριστοῦ καλό 'ναι κι ἄς τό λέμε.

5 Κάτω στά ᾿Ιεροσόλυμα καί στοῦ Χριστοῦ τόν τάφο,
ἐκεῖ κάθετ᾿ ἡ Παναγία, μόνη καί μοναχή της.
Τήν προσευχή της ἔκανε γιά τό μονογένη της.
᾿Εκεῖ πού προσευχότανε κ᾿ ἐκεῖ πού παρακαλεῖ,
'κούει οἱ βροντές καί οἱ ἀστραπές καί σύγχισες μεγάλες.

10 Βγαίνει στό παραθύρι της, θωρεῖ τή γειτονιά της.
Βλέπει τόν οὐρανό θολό, τ' ἄστρι βουρκωμένο,
τό φεγγαράκι τό λαμπρό στό αἷμα βουτηγμένο.
Πάλι ἐξανακύτταξε, βλέπει τόν ' Ἁγιο Γιάννη.
—Καλῶς τονε τό Γιάννη μου, τό μαθητή τοῦ γυιοῦ μου,
15 καί τί χαμπάρια μοὔφερες ἀπ' τό μονογενή μου;
—Κρατῶ χαμπάρια θλιβερά καί λόγια πικραμένα·
τό γυιό σου τόν ἐπιάσανε οἱ σκύλοι οἱ ' Εβραῖοι.
Σάν τἄκουσε ἡ Παναγία ἐβρέθη λιγωμένη·
ροδοσταμνό τήν ἔραιχουν ὥστε νά συνοφέρη.
20 Καί ὅταν ἐσυνόφερε τοῦτο τό λόγο λέει:
—'Ἀς ἔρθ' ἡ Μάρθα κ' ἡ Μαρία καί τοῦ Λαζάρου ἡ μάνα,
τοῦ 'Ιακώβ ἡ ἀδελφή νά πᾶμ' ὅλες ἀντάμα.

. . . .

THE VIRGIN'S LAMENT

Now it is Holy Lent, now are the holy days
when churches hold liturgies and priests chant.
And with the *kyrie eleison* and the precious words,
the lament for Christ is good; let's sing it.

5 Down in Jerusalem, at the tomb of Christ,
the Virgin is sitting all alone
saying her prayers for her only begotten Son.
And there where she is praying,
she hears thunder and lightning and great confusion.
10 She goes to her window and looks out over her neighborhood.
She sees the sky all cloudy, the stars threatening rain,
the little bright moon all bathed in blood.
She looks again and she sees Saint John.
"Welcome, John, disciple of my son.
15 What news have you brought me from my only child?"
"I have grievous news and bitter words:
those dogs, the Jews, have seized your son."
When she heard it, Mary fell into a faint;
they sprinkled rose water over her until she revived.

20   And when she had revived, she said:
"Let Martha come, and Mary and Lazarus' mother
and Jacob's sister, and let's all go together.

. . . .

Η ΗΠΕΙΡΟΣ

EPIROS

14. ΑΥΤΑ ΕΙΝΑΙ ΤΑ ΜΑΤΙΑ, ΔΗΜΟ Μ', ΤΑΜΟΡΦΑ

Μαριγούλα Ποσποτίκη καί
Ἀθανασία Ποσποτίκη
Χ. Μέτσοβον, Ἰωαννίνων

Αὐ - τά εἰν' τά μά - τια, Δῆ - μο μ', τἄ - μορ - φα, ν - αὐ -
τά εἰν' τά μά - τια, Δῆ - μο μ', τἄ - μορ - φα, Τά
φρύ - δια τά γραμ - μέ - - να, μω - ρέ
γειά σ' ἀ - γά - πη μ', γειά σου, Τά φρύ - δια τά γραμ -
μέ - να, σέ κλαῖν' τά μά - τια μου.

Αὐτά εἰν' τά μάτια, Δῆμο μ', τἄμορφα, (δίς)
τά φρύδια τά γραμμένα, μωρέ γειά σ', ἀγάπη μ', γειά σου,

τά φρύδια τά γραμμένα, σέ κλαῶ' τά μάτια μου.

. . . .

Γιά πάρε τό σπαθάκι σου καί κόψε τό λαιμό μου,
καί μάσε καί τό αἷμα μου σ' ἔνα χρυσό μαντῆλι
καί σῦρ' το στά ἐννιά χωριά, στά δέκα βιλαέτια.
5 *Κι ἄν σέ ρωτήσουν "Τί ἔχ'ς αὐτού;" "Τό αἷμα τῆς ἀγάπης."*

THESE ARE THE BEAUTIFUL EYES, DHIMO

These are the beautiful eyes, the bold eyebrows,

. . . .

Come, take your little sword and cut my throat
and gather up my blood in a gold handkerchief
and take it around to the nine villages, the ten *vilayets*.
5 And if they ask you, "What have you got there?"—"The blood of my
   love."

15. Ο ΜΕΝΟΥΣΗΣ

Μαριγούλα Ποσποτίκη
Χ. Μέτσοβον, Ἰωαννίνων

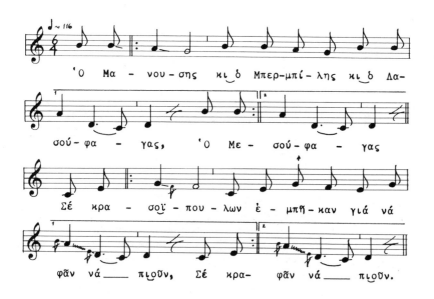

'Ο Μα - νου-σης κι ὁ Μπερ-μπί- λης κι ὁ Λα-
σού-φα - γας, 'Ο Με - σού-φα - γας
Σέ κρα - σοϊ-που-λων ἐ - μπῆ-καν γιά νά
φᾶν νά___ πιοῦν, Σέ κρα- φᾶν νά___ πιοῦν.

'Ο Μανούσης κι ὁ Μπερμπίλης κι ὁ Λασούφαγας
σέ κρασοϊπούλων ἐμπῆκαν γιά νά φᾶν νά πιοῦν.
'Κεῖ πού τρώγαν, 'κεῖ πού πίναν, 'κεῖ πού γλένταγαν,
κάτι 'πεσαν σέ κουβέντα γιά τίς ἔμορφες.
5 —Ποιά 'ν' ἡ ἄσπρη, ποιά 'ν' ἡ ρούσσα, ποιά 'ν' ἡ γαλανή,
ἡ γυναῖκα το' Μενούση εἶν' ἡ πιό καλή.
'Ὄμορφη γυναῖκα πὤχεις, βρέ Μενούσαγα.

　　–Ποῦ τήν εἶδες καί τήν ξεύρεις καί τήν 'μολογᾶς;
　　–Ψές τήν εἶδα στό πηγάδι πώπαιρνε νερό
10　καί τῆς ρίχνω τό μαντῆλι καί μοῦ τόπλυνε,
　　καί τῆς εἶπα δυό λογάκια καί τά δέχτηκε.
　　–Κι ἄν τήν εἶδες καί τήν ξεύρεις, πές μας, τί φορει;
　　–'Ασπρο ντουλουμᾶ¹ φοροῦσε, κόκκινη ποδιά,
　　γύρω-γύρω στό λαιμό της κίτρινα φλουριά.
15　Κι ὁ Μενούσης μεθυσμένος πάει, τήν ἔσφαξε·²
　　Τό πρωί, ξεμεθυσμένος, πάει τήν ἔκλαιγε·³
　　–Σήκω, ρούσσα, ἀρματόσου κ᾽ ἔμπα στό χορό
20　νά σέ δοῦν τά παλληκάρια νά σκανιάζονται,
　　νά σέ δῶ κ᾽ ἐγώ ὁ καϋμένος νά σέ χαίρομαι.

MENOUSIS

Menousis, Berbilis, and Lasoufaghas
went into a wine shop to eat and drink.
And while they were eating and drinking and enjoying themselves
the conversation turned to beautiful women.
5　"Of all the white-skinned, blonde, and blue-eyed women,
Menousis' wife is the best.
What a beautiful wife you've got, Menousagha!"
"Where did you see her that you know her and can talk about her?"
"I saw her at the well yesterday when she was drawing water,
10　and I threw her my handkerchief and she washed it,
and I said a couple of words to her and she accepted them."
"If you saw her and you know her, tell us, what does she wear?"
"She was wearing a white dress, a red apron,
and around her neck [a chain of] yellow florins."
15　So Menousis, dead drunk, went home and killed her;
in the morning, sobered up, he cried for her.
"Get up, my redhead, get dressed and go out to the dance
so the *pallikaria* can see you and go mad,
and I, poor me, so I can see you and enjoy you."

---

¹ Ντουλαμᾶς = ἐπενδύτης φουστανελοφόρου.
² "Σκότωσε" στήν δευτέρα φορά.
³ "Μίλαγε" στήν δευτέρα φορά.

16. ΠΕΝΤΕ ΜΗΝΕΣ ΠΕΡΠΑΤΟΥΣΑ

Μαριγούλα Ποσποτίκη καί
'Αθανασία Ποσποτίκη
Χ. Μέτσοβον, 'Ιωαννίνων

Πέν - τε__ μῆ - - νες περ - πα-τοῦ-σα, Πέν-τε μῆ - νες__ περ - πά-τοῦ-σα Σέ για - λό, για - λό, τό 'Δε-νά-κι μ', σέ για - λό, για - λό, [2] Κι_ᾶλ-λες

Πέντε μῆνες περπατοῦσα (δίς)
σέ γιαλό, γιαλό, τό 'Λενάκι μ', σέ γιαλό, γιαλό,

κι ἄλλες τόσες γκιξερούσα[1] στά μαυρά ἰβοννά.
Τήν ἀγάπη μου γυρεύω γιά νά τήν ἰδ ῶ.
Μέσ' στό γιουλμπαξέ[2] τήν εἶδ α πού σεργιάναγε.
5 Τά βασιλικά ποτοῦσε, τά τριαντάφυλλα.

---

[1] Γκεξερούσα = περιφερήθηκα (λ.τ. *gesmèk*).
[2] Γιούλμπαξε = κῆπον μέ τριαντάφυλλα (λ.τ. *gul bahçe*).

Μῆλο κόκκινο τῆς ρίχνω καί δέν τό δέχτηκε·
ρίχνω μάλαμα κι ἀσῆμι καί μ᾽ τό δέχτηκε.

FIVE MONTHS I ROAMED

Five months I roamed the seashore,
and as many more I wandered the black mountains
looking for my love, to see her.
I saw her in her garden, walking around,
5 watering her basil plant and her roses.
I threw her a red apple, and she rejected it;
I threw her silver and gold, and she accepted it.

17. ΣΑΡΑΝΤΑ–ΠΕΝΤΕ ΚΥΡΙΑΚΕΣ (Συρτός)

Μαριγούλα Ποσποτίκη καί
᾿Αθανασία Ποσποτίκη
Χ. Μέτσοβον, ᾿Ιωαννίνων

Σα - ράν - τα - πέν - τε__ Κυ - - ρι - α -
κές__ κ᾿ἐ-ξῆν - τα__ δυό__ Δευ - ε -
τέ - ρες __ Δέν εἶ - δα __ τήν, ἄϊ__

ἄχ, δέν__ εἶ - - δα τήν ἀ - γά - πη
μου, ν-ἀ - μάν, δέν__ εἶ - - - δα
τήν__ ἀ - γά - πη __ μου, [2] Δέν εἶ - δα

Σαράντα-πέντε Κυριακές κ᾽ ἑξῆντα-δυό Δευτέρες
δέν εἶδα τή, ἀι ἄχ, δέν εἶδα τήν ἀγάπη μου,
ν-ἀμάν, δέν εἶδα τήν ἀγάπη μου,

δέν εἶδα τήν ἀγάπη μου, τήν ἀγαπητικιά μου.
Μιά Κυριακίτσα τό πρωί τήν εἶδα στολισμένη
μέ δυό μαντήλια στό λαιμό καί τέσσαρα στήν πλάτη.
5   Καί μέ τό μάτι τῆς πατῶ καί μέ τ᾽ ἀχείλ᾽ τῆς λέω:
—Ποῦ ἤσουν ἐψές, ποῦ ἤσουν προψές [. . .]
—Ν-ἐψές ἤμουν στήν μάνα μου, προψές στήν ἀδελφή μου
κι ἀπόψε θἄμαστε τά δυό, τά δυό τ᾽ ἀγαπημένα.
Σώχω ψαράκια στό ταψί καί περδίκια ψημένα,
10 σώχω κ᾽ ἕνα γλυκό κρασί.

FORTY-FIVE SUNDAYS (*Syrtos* dance)

Forty-five Sundays and sixty-two Mondays
I hadn't seen my love, my beloved.
One little Sunday morning I saw her all dressed up
with two scarves 'round her neck and four down her back.
5   I run over her with my eyes, and I say to her with my lips:
"Where were you yesterday and the day before?"
"Yesterday I was at my mother's; the day before my sister's;
and tonight we'll be two lovers.
I've got some little fish in the pan and roasted partridge,
10 and I've got a good sweet wine."

18. ΘΕΛΗΣΑ ΝΑ ΚΑΝΩ ΓΙΟΥΡΓΙΑ

Μαριγούλα Ποσποτίκη
Χ. Μέτσοβον, Ἰωαννίνων

"Αχ, θέ-λη - σα ___ νά κά-νω
γιούρ-για ___ στήν πο -
διά ___ σου τήν ___ και -
νούρ - - - για. Γιούρ - - για,
γιούρ - για Στήν πο - διά σου τήν και-νούρ - - για.
Γιούρ - - - για, γιούρ - - - για Στά πα -
λιά ___ καί στά ___ και - νούρ - - για.

' Ἄχ, θέλησα νά κάνω γιούργια[1]
στήν ποδιά σου τήν καινούργια.
Γιούργια, γιούργια, στήν ποδιά σου τήν καινούργια.
Γιούργια, γιούργια, στά παληά καί στά καινούργια.

' Ἄχ, θέλησα νά κάνω μάκια
στό λαιμό, λαιμό καί στά ματάκια.
Μάκια, μάκια, μάκια στά ματάκια.
Μάκια, μάκια, λαιμό καί στά ματάκια.

I WANTED TO ATTACK

I wanted to attack
your new apron.

I wanted to leave marks
on your neck and your little eyes.

[1] Γιούργια = γιουρρούσι.

19. ΠΕΡΑ Σ'ΕΚΕΙΝΟ ΤΟ ΒΟΥΝΟ

Μαριγούλα Ποσποτίκη
Χ. Μέτσοβον, Ἰωαννίνων

Πέρα σ' ἐκεῖνο τό ἰβουνό, πέρα σ' ἐκεῖ τή ράχη,
ἄχ, ν-ἐκεῖ εἶν' ὁ πῦ-, ν-ὁ πύργος γιαλινός,
ν-ἀμάν, ἐκεῖ εἶν' ὁ πῦ-, ν-ὁ πύργος γιαλινός,

ν-ἐκεῖ εἰν' ὁ πῦργος γιαλινός μέ κρυσταλένια τζάμια.
N̄-ἐκεῖ κοιμᾶται μιά ξανθιά, ξανθιά καί μαυρομάτα.
Τό πῶς νά τή ξυπνίσωμε, τό πῶς νά τῆς τό ἰποῦμε;
5 —Ξύπνα, καϋμέν' Ἀναστασᾶ, ξύπνα καί μήν κοιμᾶσαι.
Τό πῶς μᾶς πῆρ' ἡ χαραυγή, τό δάλιο μεσημέρη.
—Τό πῶς νά σηκοθῶ, λεβέντη μου [. . .]
Μπερδεύκαν τά μαλλάκια μου μαζύ μέ τά δικά σου.
—Σήκω ν' ἀνάψης τή φωτιά.

OVER THERE ON THAT MOUNTAIN

Over there on that mountain, over there on that ridge,
there's a castle facing the sea, with crystal window panes.
A blonde girl is sleeping there, blonde with black eyes.
How can we wake her, how can we tell her?
5 "Wake up, poor Anastasha, wake up, don't sleep.
Look how dawn overtook us, the torch of midday."
"How can I get up, *levendi*?
My hair is all entangled with your own."
"Get up and light the fire."

20. ΚΟΡΗ ΠΟΥ ΠΑΣ ΣΤΟΝ ΠΟΤΑΜΟ

Μαριγούλα Ποσποτίκη καί
Ἀθανασία Ποσποτίκη
Χ. Μέτσοβον, Ἰωαννίνων

Κόρη, καλέ, κόρη πού πᾶς στόν ποταμό,
κόρη πού πᾶς στόν ποταμό, Ἑλένη, γιά νά πλύνης,
πάρε κ᾽ἐμέ τά ροῦχα μου, Ἑλένη, μήν τ᾽ἀφύης.

Νά μήν τά πλύνης μέ νερό, μόν' μέ τά δακρυά σου
καί μέ τό μοσκοσάπουνο πού λούζεις τά μαλλιά σου.

5   Νά μήν τ' ἀπλώσης σέ δεντρί οὐδέ καί σέ κλωνάρι,
μόνο σέ πικρομύγδαλια π' ἀνθίζει τό Γεννάρη.

Νά πέσουν φύλλα επάνω σου, τά ἄνθη στήν ποδιά σου,
νά πέσουν πικρομύγδαλα γλυκά στήν ἀγκαλιά σου.

WHEN YOU GO TO THE RIVER

When you go to the river to wash, Eleni,
take my clothes, too, Eleni, don't leave them.

And don't wash them with water, but only with your tears
and with the musk soap you wash your hair with.

5   And don't spread them on a tree or a branch,
but only on the bitter-almond tree that blooms in January,

so the leaves can fall on you, the blossoms in your apron,
so the bitter almonds can fall sweetly into your lap.

21. ΚΑΛΑΝΤΑ ΤΩΝ ΧΡΙΣΤΟΥΓΕΝΝΩΝ

Μαριγούλα Ποσποτίκη
Χ. Μέτσοβον, Ἰωαννώων

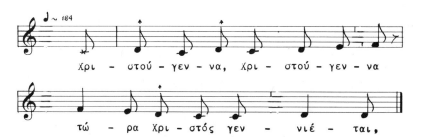

Χρι - στού - γεν - να, Χρι - στού - γεν - να

τώ - ρα Χρι - στός γεν - νιέ - ται,

Γύρισμα

Κό - λιν-τρα, μέ- λιν-τρα, γειά χα - ρά κα'

τοῦ πα - σᾶ, Τσίν-τσίν κά - κά, δω'μ' τά κου-

λά - κια, τά θύ - ρα τά τσα - νάκ Κου-

λιν - τε, μί - λιν-τε, γειά χα - ρά καλ' μέ- ρα,

Ντόι-κου-λα κολ - τέ - τα, μπλάμ τά πού - σα.

Χριστούγεννα, Χριστούγεννα, τώρα Χριστός γεννιέται,
γεννιέται καί βαφτίζεται στούς οὐρανούς ἀπάνω.
Καί ὅλοι-ὅλοι χαίρουνται κι ὅλοι δοξολογοῦνε.
Μέ τά λεμόνια φλίγονται[1] γιατ' ὁ Χριστός γεννιέται.
5 Ἰούδας ἔπρεπε νά λέ' "Τί μ' ἔβαλες ἀπάνω;"
Κατέβα Γιάννη, Δέσποινα γιά δά νά μᾶς φιλέψης.
Σήκω κυρά, σήκω κυρά, γιά κάνε τήν τιμή σου,
νά μᾶς φιλέψης τίποτα καί φέτο καί τοῦ χρό-

Γύρισμα
Κόλωτρα[2] μέλωτρα, γειά χαρά κα' τοῦ πασᾶ,
10 τσών τσών κά κά, δ ω' μ' τά κουλάκια,[3]
τά θύρα τά τσανακ[4]
Κούλωτε[5] μιλωτε, γειά χαρά, καλ' μέρα,
ντοϊκουλα κοσέντα, μπλάμ τά πουσᾶ.

KALANDA FOR CHRISTMAS

Christmas, Christmas, now Christ is born,
born and baptized in the heavens above.
And everyone is glad, and everyone is singing praises.
[The demons are grieving] because Christ is born.
5 Judas should be saying: "Why did you set me up on high?"
Come down, John and Virgin Mary, and treat us.
Get up, lady, come do what's honorable,
give us something and good luck this year and next.

---

[1] Καί τά δαιμόνια θλίβονται (βλ. Γιαγκᾶ, *Ἠπειρωτικά Δημοτικά Τραγούδια*, 203).
[2] Κόλωτρα = κάλαντα.
[3] Δηλ., δῶσε μου τά κουλούρια.
[4] Δηλ., τήν πόρτα τήν κτίπισα.
[5] Κούλωτε = κάλαντα.

Yirisma:

Kalanda,——, health and joy even to the pasha,
10   ——, give me the *koulouria*,
I knocked at your door.
Kalanda,——, health and joy, good morning, ——.

22. Η ΒΑΣΙΛΑΡΧΟΝΤΙΣΣΑ

Γιώργιος Τσέτσος
Χ. Μέτσοβον, Ἰωαννίνων

Δέν εἶ - ναι κρῖ - μα, ἄχ, κι ἄ-δε - κο, ___ Βα -

σι - - λα - ἀρ-χον - - τισ - σα,

δέν ___ εἶ - ναι κι ἀ - μαρ-τί - α, [2] Νά -

α εἶ-ν' ἡ Βα - - σι - - λω, Βα - - - -

, σ' ἐ - - - - - ρε - - μιά,

Δέν εἶναι κρῖμα, ἄχ, κι ἄδεκο, Βασιλαρχόντισσα, δέν εἶναι κι ἀμαρτία,
Νά εἶν' ἡ Βασέλω, Βάσω μ', σ' ἐρεμιά, στά κλέφτικα λεμέρια,
νά στρώνε πεύκα, Βάσω μ', στρώματα, ὠρέ, ν-ὀξυές προσκεφαλάκια,

Κι ὸ Θύμιος Γάκης, <u>Βάσω μ'</u>, στό πλευρό, κρυφά τήν κοβεντιάξει:
5 —Ξύπνα Βασέλω, <u>Βάσω μ'</u>, γιατ' ἔφεξε, ωρέ, ν-ἡ Πουλιά πάει ἔγιωμα,
ξύπνα νά πάρε τό, <u>Βάσω μ'</u>, τόν καφέ, ωρέ, νά πάρε τό λοκούμι.
Ν-ἐξαγορά, <u>Δόκο μ'</u>, μας σέ ϑᾶσαι, 'πε το, Νικολανίτσα

. . . .

. . . .

VASILO, THE *ARKHONDISSA*

Isn't it wrong and unjust, isn't it a sin
for Vasilo to be up on the wild mountains, in the *klefts'* hideouts,
spreading pine branches for a mattress, beech leaves for pillows;
and Thimios Ghakis at her side whispering:
5 "Wake up, Vasilo, it's dawn, the Pleiades have gone, it's morning,
wake up and drink your coffee, eat a *loukoumi*.
You're going to be held for ransom, accept it, Nikolanitsa,

. . . .

. . . .

23. Η ΠΕΡΙΣΤΕΡΟΥΛΑ

Γιώργιος Τσέτσος
Χ. Μέτσοβον, Ἰωαννίνων

'Ω - ρέ ποῦ ἦ - σουν Πε - - ρε-,____ Πε -

ρι - στε - - ε - ρού - λα   μου . . .

[2] Στούς κά - μπους ἦ-, μά - να, στούς κά - μπους ἦ - μουν

μά - να,   κ'έ - - - - - βοσ - κα

στά   πλα - για____ γκε-, βρέ, γκε - ζε -

ροῦ - ου - σα, [3] Καί τ'ὀ - - - - ρα -

α - τό, μά - - να μ', ____ καί τ'ὀ - ρα - τό, μά-

να, στη - ε - νό - που - - - - ρο

—Ὠρέ, ποῦ ἤσουν Περε-, Περιστερούλα μου,
τόσον καιρό, μάνα μ', χαμένη;
—Στούς κάμπους ἤ-, μάνα, στούς κάμπους ἤμουν, μάνα, κ' ἔβοσκα,
στά πλάγια γκε-, βρέ, γκεξερούσα,¹
Καί τ' ὀρατό, μάνα μ', καί τ' ὀρατό, μάνα, στενόπουρο
σμά τ' 'Αγιο, στ' 'Αγιο Δημῆτρι
πῆγα νά μά-, μάνα μ', πῆγα νά μά-, νά μάσω κάστανα
μέ τ' ἄλλα τά, μάνα μου, τά κορίτσα.
5 Καί οἱ κλέφτες, μάνα μ', καί οἱ κλέφτες μᾶ', βρέ, μᾶς ἀγνάντεψαν
ὠρέ, ν-ἀπό ψελή, ψελή ραχούλα.
"Κορίτσα κα-, βρέ, καστανότεκα,
ἐλᾶτε πα-, μάνα μου, παραπάνω·
κάτι νά σᾶ', μάνα μ', κάτι νά σᾶ', νά σᾶς ρωτήσουμε,
δυό λόγια νά, μάνα μ', νά σᾶς ποῦμε.
Μήνα εἶναι Τοῦ-, μάνα μ', μήνα εἶναι Τοῦ-, βρέ, Τοῦρκοι στό χωριό;
Μήνα εἶναι κι 'Α-, μάνα μου, κι 'Αρβανίτες;"
"Ν-ἐμεῖς, παιδιά, ν-ἐμεῖς, παιδιά, παιδιά, δέν ξεύρομε."

PERISTEROULA

"Where have you been gone for so long, Peristeroula?"
"I was at the pastures tending the sheep, I was wandering around the hills,

---

¹ Γκεξερούσα = περιφερήθηκα (λ.τ. *gesmèk*).

and that narrow pass on the ridge, next to the Saint Dhimitri chapel,
I went there to gather chestnuts with the other girls.
5   And some *klefts* were watching us from a high ridge:
'Come up a little higher, chestnut girls,
we've got something to ask you, we want a word or two with you.
Are there any Turks in the village, any Albanians?'
'*Pedhia*, we don't know.'"

24. Η ΒΑΓΓΕΛΙΤΣΑ

Γιώργιος Τσέτσος
Χ. Μέτσοβον, Ἰωαννίνων

Ἔνας ροῦσσος καβά-να-λλα (δίς)
   ροῦσσος κ' ἔμορφος, Βαγγελίτσα, ροῦσσος κ' ἔμορφος
Καβάλλα περπατοῦ-νο-σε (δίς)
   κι ὅλο τραγουδάει, Βαγγελίτσα, κι ὅλο τραγουδάει.
Ἀκμε τό νοῦ του, 'λε-νε-γε: (δίς)
   —Νά εἶχα πρόβατα, Βαγγελλίτσα, νά ἤμου' τσέλιγκα'.
Νά εἶχα καί χίλια γί-νε-δια (δίς)

χίλια πρόβατα, Βαγγελίτσα, να ήμουν τσέλιγκας.
5 Νἀχα ἕναν τυρου-νου-γκᾶ (δίς)
σέ ἐψηλό ἰβουνό, Βαγγελίτσα, σέ ἐψηλό ἰβουνό.
Νά εἰχα ἕναν γλυκό γά-να-λα (δίς)
καί γλυκό τυρί, Βαγγελίτσα μ', καί γλυκό τυρί.
Νά ἦταν καί πανεγύ-νι-ρι (δίς)
κάθε κεριακή, Βαγγελίτσα μ', κάθε κεριακή.
Νά ἦρθε καί Βαγγελί-νι-τσα (δίς)
νά κερνάει κρασί, Βαγγελίτσα, νά κερνάει κρασί.

VANGELITSA

A handsome red-haired man on horseback,
riding and singing.
His mind works and he says: "I wish I had some sheep,
I wish I had a thousand goats and a thousand sheep,
5 I wish I had a cheeseworks up on a high mountain,
I wish I had sweet milk and sweet cheese,
I wish there were a festival every Sunday
so Vangelitsa could come and serve the wine."

25. Ο ΠΝΕΥΜΑΤΙΚΟΣ

Γιώργιος Τσέτσος
Χ. Μέτσοβον, Ἰωαννίνων

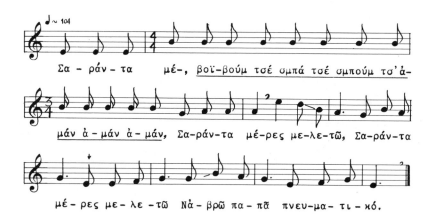

Σα - ράν - τα   μέ-, βοϊ-βούμ τσέ ομπά τσέ ομπούμ τσ'ἀ-

μάν ἀ - μάν ἀ - μάν, Σα-ράν-τα μέ-ρες με-λε-τῶ, Σα-ράν-τα

μέ- ρες με- λε -τῶ Νά - βρῶ πα - πᾶ πνευ-μα- τι - κό.

Σαράντα μέ-, βοϊβούμ τσέ σμπά τσέ σμπούμ τσ' ἀμάν ἀμάν ἀμάν
Σαράντα μέρες μελετῶ (δίς)
νὰβρῶ παπᾶ πνευματικό.

Κι ἀπάνω στά σαράντα-δυό
βρίσκω καί τό πνευματικό.

5   —Παπᾶ μου ξεμούλογά με
τά κρίματά μου ρῶτα με.

—Τά κρίματά σου εἶναι πολλά
κι ἀγάπη νά μή πιάσης πιά.

—Κι άν άρνεστῆς ἐσύ παπᾶ
10 τόν ἄρτο καί τή λειτουργιά,

Τότε θά ν-ἀρνεστῶ κ' ἐγώ
δυό μαῦρα μάτια π' ἀγαπῶ.

Πάει ὁ παπᾶς στήν ἐκκλησά,
πάγω κ' ἐγώ στήν παπαδιά.

15 Πάει ὁ παπᾶς στίς ὧρες του,
πάγω κ' ἐγώ στίς κόρες του.

THE CONFESSOR

Forty days I looked
for a priest for confession.

And after forty-two days
I found a confessor.

5 "Father, confess me;
ask me my sins."

"Your sins are many;
you must not pursue love anymore."

"Father, if you renounce
10 your holy bread and your liturgy

then I'll renounce
the two black eyes that I love."

So the priest goes off to the church,
and I go off to his wife.

15 The priest goes off to his hours,
and I go off to his daughters.

26. ΚΑΛΑΝΤΑ ΤΟΥ ΛΑΖΑΡΟΥ

Εὐάγγελος Τόζολος, Δημήτριος
Γάτσος, Παρασκευή ' Εξάρτου,
' Ελευθερία Σταμούλη, Εὐδοκία
Παπᾶ
Χ. Ζίτσα, 'Ιωαννίνων

[5] Κι αὐ-τά τά λα-γα-ρίσ-μα-τα τά δέ-νω στό μαν-τῆ-λι·

Τό μικρό μικρούτσικο π' ὅτα' στό γέννα ἡ μάνα,
κ' ἐγώ στήν θύρα στέκομαι, Θεό παρακαλοῦσα:
—Θεέ μ', νά γίνω βασιληᾶς, Θεέ μ', νά γίνω ρῆγας,
νά κοσκινίζω τό φλουρί, νά πέφτη τό λογάρι.
5 Κι αὐτά τά λαγαρίσματα τά δένω στό μαντῆλι·
καί τό μαντῆλι στό σπαθί καί τό σπαθί στή ζώση·
κ' ἡ ζώση ἀπάνω στ' ἄλογο καί τ' ἄλογο στούς κάμπους.
Διψοῦν οἱ κάμποι γιά νερό καί τά βουνά γιά χιόνια·
διψάει κ' ἐμένα ὁ γρίβας μου γιά δροσερό ποτάμι.

KALANDA FOR LAZARUS DAY

The little tiny baby, when his mother gave birth to him,
I was standing at the door, praying to God:

God, let me become a king,
so I can sift florins and let the treasure fall through,
5   so I can wrap the pieces of pure gold in a kerchief
and put the kerchief on the sword and the sword in the belt
and the belt on the horse and the horse over the plains.
The plains thirst for water and the mountains for snow,
and my grey horse thirsts for the cool river.

27. ΜΕ ΓΕΛΑΣΑΝ ΤΑ ΠΟΥΛΙΑ

Καλιόπη Οἰκονομίδου
Χ. Μονοδέντρι, Ζαγορίου

2 Μέ γέ-λα-σαν καί μοῦ εἴ-πα-νε _____

ὁ Χά-ρος δέν μέ παί-αιρ - - - νει _____.

Βά-ζω φτιά-νω, ὠ - - - - - - - ι-

μέ, _____ βά-ζω φτιά-

νω _____ τά σπί-τια _____ μου,

Γύρισμα

'Α-έ-ρας θά _____ τά - - α-ρά -

Μέ γέλασαν[ε] τά πουλιά, τῆς ἄνοιξης τ' ἀηδόνια,
<u>'Άχ</u>, μέ γέλασαν, <u>μέ γέλασαν</u> καί μοῦ ἔπανε,

Μέ γέλασαν καί μοῦ εἴπανε ὁ Χάρος δέν μέ παίρνει.
Βάζω, φτιάνω, <u>ωιμέ</u>, βάζω φτιάνω τά σπίτια μου,

Βάζω, φτιάνω τά σπίτια μου, τά μαρμαροκτισμένα·
<u>'Άχ</u>, βάζω στίς πόρ-, <u>ωιμέ</u>, βάζω στίς πόρτες μάλαμα,

    <u>Γύρισμα:</u>
    Ἀέρας θά ταράξη τά πλατανόφυλλα· <u>τρια-λα-λα-λα-λα-λα-λα</u>,
    Θεός νά τά φυλάχη τά Ἑλληνόπουλα, <u>μπομπόμ</u>, τά Ἑλληνόπουλα.

Βάζω στίς πόρτες μάλαμα, στά παραθύρια ἀσῆμι,
<u>'αχ</u>, καί στά παρα-, <u>ωιμέ</u>, καί στά παραθυρόφυλλα,

5 <u>Καί στά παραθυρόφυλλα</u> ὁλομαργαριτάρι.
Βλέπω τό Χάρ-, <u>ωιμέ</u>, βλέπω τό Χάρο νἄρχεται

Γύρισμα:

Τό ἕνα, δυό, τρία καί τ᾽ ἄλλο τέσσαρα, τρια-λα-λα-λα-λα-λα-λα
Ζωή πού τήν περνᾶμε ἡμεῖς τά 'λευθερά, μπομπόμ, ἡμεῖς τά
ἠλευθερά

Βλέπω τό Χάρο νἄρχεται στόν κάμπο καβαλλάρι·
σέρνει τούς νιούς ἀπ᾽ τά μαλλιά, τούς γέρους ἀπ᾽ τά γένια.
Σέρνει μιά κόκκινη μηλιά στά μῆλα φορτομένα.
—᾽Άφες με, Χάρου μ᾽, τ᾽ αφες με, τά νιάτα μου λυπήσου.
10   Τά νιάτα δέ λυπήθηκε.

Γύρισμα:

Διαμάντι δαχτυλίδι φορεῖς στό χέρι σου,
κι ἀπάνω γράφει πέτρα: "νά ζῆς τό ταίρι σου."

THE BIRDS LAUGHED AT ME

The birds laughed at me, the nightingales of spring,
they laughed at me and told me that Charon would never take me.
So I set my marble houses in order—
I put gold on the doors, silver on the windows,
5   and pearls all over the shutters.
[And now] I see Charon riding over the plain,
leading youths by their hair, old men by their beards,
and carrying a red-apple tree laden with apples.
"Leave me alone, Charon, pity my youth."
10   He didn't pity my youth.

28. Η ΓΡΙΑ ΤΖΑΒΕΛΙΝΑ

Καλιόπη Οἰκονομίδου
Χ. Μονοδένδρι, Ζαγορίου

Κο-ρί-τσα 'πό τά _____ Γιάν - - - νι -
να, _____ Ἡ γρι-ά Τζα -
βέ-, Τζα-βέ-λι - - - να,
'Ωρ' νυ-φά-δες ἀπ' τό Σού - λι, Τά μαῦ-ρα
νά, _____ μπρέ, νά φο - ρέ - σι - - τε,

Κορίτσα 'πό τά Γιάννινα, ἡ γριά Τζαβέ-, Τζαβέλινα,
  ὠρ' νυφάδες ἀπ' τό Σούλι,
τά μαῦρα νά, μπρέ, νά φορέσιτε,

στά μαῦρα νά ντυϑῆτε·
τό Σοῦλι χαρατσόϑηκε,[1] χαράτσι νά πληρώσῃ.
Τζαβέλινα σάν τἄκουσε βαρεά τῆς κακοφάνει.
5 Παίρνει καί ζώνει τό σπαϑί καί τά χρυσά τσαπράκια,[2]
καί περνεῖ δίπλα τά βουνά, διπλά τά κορφόνια.
Σφυρίζει μιά, σφυρίζει δυό, σφυρίζει τρεῖς κι πέντε.
Τά παλληκάρια φϑάσανε, πόλεμο γιά νά πιάσουν.
Τά βάζει ὅλα στήν γραμμή.

OLD TZAVELINA

Women of Yiannina, brides of Souli,
put on your mourning clothes, dress yourselves in black:
Souli is being taxed, she's to pay a Turkish tax.
Soon as she heard about it, Tzavelina was greatly offended.
5 She puts on her sword and her gold greaves,
she goes to the mountains, to the peaks,
she whistles once, twice, three times, and five times.
The *pallikaria* arrived, ready to make war.
She sets them all in a line.

---

[1] Χαρατσόϑηκε = ἔπρεπε νά πληρόνῃ χαράτσι ἡ φόρος (λ.τ. *haraç*).
[2] Τσαπράξια.

29. ΤΟΥ ΧΑΤΖΗΜΙΧΑΗΛ ΟΙ ΑΝΙΨΑ

Ἰωάννης Ροὔντας
Χ. Βίτσα, Ζαγορίου

Ὠρέ το' Χατζῆ' α' οἱ ἀνηψά ὀρηγάθηγκαν θῆλα.[1]
—Γιά ἰδέστ' καμάρα πὤσερνε

Γιά ἰδέστ' καμάρα πὤσερνε, καμάρι ὄπο' σύρει,
κι ἀπό φλωρί δέν φαίνεται κι ἀπό μαργαριθάρι.[2]
Κ'οἱ κλέφτες τήν ἀγνάντιψαν, πᾶ' σάν γιά νά τήν πάρου'.
5   —Σταθῆτει, λέει, 'φεντάδες μου, σταθῆτε παλληκάρια,
ν' ἀλυσοδέσω τό παιδί, νά τό χορτάσω γάλα,
νά τό χορτάσω φιλιμα.

[1] Θῆλυς ἡ κόρη.
[2] Μαργαριτάρι.

KHATZIMIKHAIL'S NEPHEWS

Khatzimikhail's nephews were coveting a young woman.
"Look at the *kamara* walking there
almost hidden by all her gold florins and pearls."
And the *klefts* stared at her and went to take her.
5   "Wait, *afendadhes*," she said, "wait, *pallikaria*,
let me tie up the child first and give him his fill of milk
and give him his fill of kisses."

30. Ο ΓΙΑΚΑΣ

Ἰωάννης Ρούντας
Χ. Βίτσα, Ζαγορίου

Καί σεῖς βου-νά, βου-νά τοῦ Γρε - βέ - νου____

____ καί πεύ-κα τοῦ____ Με - τσό-βου____ Λί - γο____

νά χα-,____ νά χα - μη - λώ - σα - - τε,

K' ἐσεῖς βουνά, βουνά τοῦ Γρεβένου καί πεύκα τοῦ Μετσόβου,
Λίγο νά χα-, νά χαμηλώσατε,

λίγο νά χα-, νά χαμηλώσατε 'να ντουφέκι μέλον[1]
γιά να φάνο', Γιάκα μ', τά Γριβένα

γιά νά φάνο', Γιάκα μ', τά Γριβενά κι αὐτό τό Μέγα Σπήλιο,
πώς πολεμοῦ', Γιάκα μ', οἱ Ἕλληνες,

πώς πολεμοῦ', Γιάκα μ', οἱ Ἕλληνες σ'αὐτό τό Μέγα Σπήλιο.
5   Βάστα καϋμέ-, καϋμένε Θόδορε.

[1] Ἕνα τουφέκι μέρος.

YIAKIS

You mountains of Ghrevena and pines of Metsovon,
lower yourselves a little, the length of a rifle shot
so Ghrevena and Megha Spilio will appear,
the Greeks fighting at Megha Spilio.
5   Hold fast, *kaimene* Thodhore.

31. Η ΠΟΤΑΜΙΑ

Ἰωάννης Ροὺντας
Χ. Βίτσα, Ζαγορίου

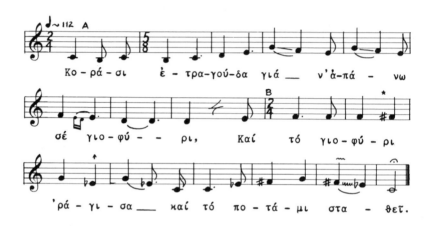

Κο - ρά - σι   ἐ - τρα-γού-δα   γιά ___   ν᾿ ἀ-πά - νω   σέ   γιο - φύ - - ρι,   Καί   τό   γιο-φύ - ρι   ᾿ρά - γι - σα ___   καί   τό   πο - τά - μι   στα - θεῖ.

Κοράσι ἐτραγούδα γιά ν᾿ ἀπάνω σέ γιοφύρι,
καί τό γιοφύρι ᾿ράγισε καί τό ποτάμι σταθεῖ.
—Κόρη, μή ἀπάψῃ τόν ἀχώ[1] καί πάρ᾿ κι ἄλλο τραγοῦδι.
—Καί πῶς ν᾿ ἀπάψω τόν ἀχώ νά πῶ κι ἄλλο τραγοῦδι;
5 ᾿Έχω τόν ἄντρα μ᾿ ἄρρωστο καί γιατρικό γυρεύω.
—Νά πιάσῃς στρούγγα[2] τοῦ λαγοῦ, τό γάλα του ν᾿ ἀρμέξῃς.
Κι ἄμαν θά γέν᾿ τό γιατρικό τόν ἄντρα νά γυρέψῃς.

. . . .

[1] Ἠχώ.
[2] Στρούγγα = ποιμνιοστάσιον.

AT THE RIVER

A young woman was singing on a bridge,
and the bridge cracked and the river stopped.
"*Kori*, why don't you stop that noise and sing another song?"
"How can I stop this noise and sing another song?
5   I have a sick husband, and I'm looking for a cure for him."
"Find a den of rabbits and milk one,
and when the medicine is ready, go to your husband."

. . . .

Η ΜΑΚΕΔΟΝΙΑ

MACEDONIA

32. ΕΝΑΣ ΛΕΒΕΝΤΗΣ ΧΟΡΕΥΕ

Νικόλαος Τετραμιδας
Χ. Παλατιανό, Κιλκίς

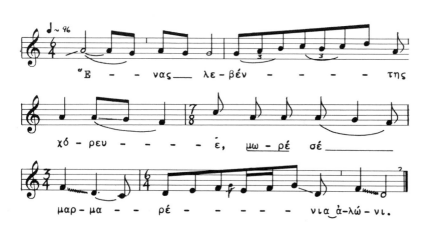

Ἕνας λεβέντης χόρευε, μωρέ, σέ μαρμαρένια ἀλώνι.

Κ' ἡ κόρη πού τόν ἀγαπᾶ κ' ἡ κόρη πού τόν θέλει,
μέ τῶνα μάτι τούκανε καί μέ τ' ἀχειλ' τοῦ λέει:
—Ποῦσουν' ἐψές, λεβέντη μου, ποῦσουν προψές τό βράδυ;
5   —Εψές ἤμουν' στή μάνα μου, προψές στήν ἀδελφή μου,
κι ἀπόψε, μαυρομάτα μου, θαρθῶ στή καμαρά σου.

A *LEVENDI* WAS DANCING

A *levendi* was dancing on a marble threshing floor.
And the girl who loves him, the girl who wants him,
signals him with one eye and says to him with her lips:
"Where were you last night, *levendi*, where were you the night
    before?"
5   "Last night I was at my mother's; the night before my sister's;
    and tonight, my black eyes, I'll come into your bedroom."

33. ΤΑ ΜΑΓΙΑ

'Ανδρέας Ζαραλῆς
Χ. Παλατιανό, Κιλκίς

Ποιά νὰν αὐτή πού μουριξε, μωρέ, τὰ μάγια στό πηγάδι;
καί μάγεψε τόν ἄνδρα μου καί θέλει νά τόν πάρη;
Μήν τά πιστεύης, ἄνδρα μου, τὰ μάγια πού σοῦ κάνουν·
ἄλλων τά πιστέψης, ἄνδρα μου, ἐσύ θά μετανοιώσης.
5 'Εγώ στίς τρεῖς[1] θά λούξω, στίς τέσσερες θ' ἀλλάξω,
καί μέσ' στίς δεκατέσσερες ν-ἄλλον ἄνδρα θά πάρω.

THE BEWITCHING

Who was it who cast a spell on me at the well?
She's bewitched my husband, and she wants to marry him.
Don't believe the magic they've worked on you, husband—
if you believe it, you'll regret it.
5 On the third [day] I'll wash, on the fourth I'll change,
and on the fourteenth I'll take another husband.

[1] Δηλ., τρεῖς ἡμέρες.

34. ΒΡΥΣΗ ΜΟΥ ΜΑΛΑΜΑΤΕΝΙΑ

Ἀνδρέας Ζαραλῆς
Χ. Παλατιανό, Κιλκίς

'Ω - ρέ, βρύ-ση ___ μου μα - - λα- μα - - τέ - νι α,

Ὠρέ, βρύση μου μαλαματένια,
ὠρέ, πῶς βαστᾶς κρυό νερό;
Ὠρέ, πῶς βαστῶ κ᾽ ἐγώ ὁ καϋμένος,
ὠρέ, τῆς ἀγάπης τόν καϋμό;

Νάμουν βρύση, νάμουν στέρνα, νάμουν γάργαρο νερό,
νά σοῦ πλένω τά χεράκια καί τόν ἄσπρο σου λαιμό.

MY GOLD FOUNTAIN

Gold fountain, how do you hold cool water?
Poor me, how do I endure the sorrow of love?

I wish I were a fountain or a cistern or clear swirling water
so I could wash your little hands and your white neck.

35. ΜΙΑ ΚΟΚΚΙΝΟΦΟΡΕΜΕΝΗ

Παναγιώτα Ζαραλῆ
Χ. Παλατιανό, Κιλκίς

Μιά κοκκι-, καλέ μάνα μου,
μιά κοκκινοφορεμένη (δίς)
μοΰχει τήν καρδιά κα᾽μένη.

Πῶς νᾶκα-, καλέ μάνα μου,
πῶς νᾶκανα νά τή γελάσω, (δίς)
τό χεράκι της νά πιάσω;

5 Στό χορό, καλέ γιόκα μου,
στό χορό νά πού χορεύει, (δίς)
σῦρε, πιάσ᾽ την ἀπ᾽ τό χέρι.

Κι ἄν τή δῆς, καλέ γιόκα μου,
κι ἄν τή δῆς καί κάνει πέρα,
ἀπαράτα την καί φεύγα.

A GIRL IN A RED DRESS

"Mother, a girl in a red dress
has burned my heart.

How can I trick her
and catch hold of her little hand?"

5 "Son, at the dance where she's dancing,
take the lead and catch her by the hand.

And if you see her and she turns away,
leave her and go."

36. ΣΟΥ ΕΙΠΑ, ΜΑΝΑ, ΠΑΝΔΡΕΨΕ ΜΕ

Παναγιώτα Ζαραλῆ
Χ. Παλατιανό, Κιλκίς

Σοῦ εἶπα, μά-, καλέ μάνα μου,
σο' εἶπα, μάνα, πάνδρεψέ με, (δίς)
σπιτονοικοκύρεψέ με.

Καὶ στά ξένα μή μέ δώσης,
γιατί θά τό μετανοιώσης.

5 Ἐγώ στά ξένα θ' ἀρρωστήσω,
τί μανόλα[1] μ' θά ζητέσω;

Θά ζητήσω τήν κονιάδα[2]
καί τήν πρώτη συννεφάδα,

ἡ κονιάδα μ' τά πρεκιά[3] της,
10 ἡ συννεφάδα μ' τά παιδιά της.

I TOLD YOU, MOTHER, MARRY ME OFF

I told you mother, marry me off,
make me a housewife.

But don't give me away into a foreign country,
or you'll regret it.

5 In a foreign country I'll get sick,
and who will I ask for?

---

[1] Μανούλα.
[2] Κουνιάδα.
[3] Προικιά.

I'll have to ask for my *kouniadha*
and the elder *sinnefadha*,

my *kouniadha* with her dowry,
10 my *sinnefadha* with her children.

37. Η ΠΑΝΑΓΙΩΤΟΥΛΑ

Παναγιώτα Ζαραλῆ
Χ. Παλατιανό, Κιλκίς

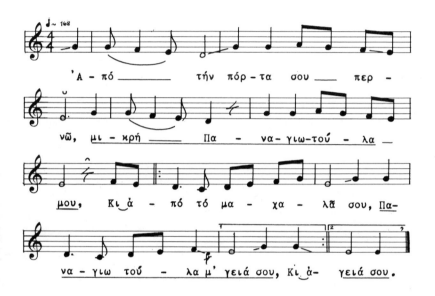

'Α - πό ____ τήν πόρ - τα σου ____ περ -
νῶ, μι - κρή ____ Πα - να - γιω-τού - λα ____
μου, Κι ἀ - πό τό μα - χα - λᾶ σου, Πα-
να - γιω τού - λα μ᾽ γειά σου, Κι ἀ- γειά σου.

᾽Από τήν πόρτα σου περνῶ, μικρή Παναγιωτούλα μου,
κι ἀπό τό μαχαλᾶ σου, Παναγιωτούλα μ᾽, γειά σου.

Κι ἄκουσα πού σέ μάλωναν, ἡ μάνα κ᾽ ἡ θειά σου.
Κι ἄν μέ[1] μάλωνα᾽ πού περνῶ νά μήν ξαναπεράσω.

_____
[1] Σέ.

PANAYIOTOULA

I pass by your door and through your neighborhood,
and I heard them scolding you, your mother and your aunt.
If they were scolding you because I pass by, I won't pass by again.

Tsakisma:
My little Panayiotoula,
My Panayiotoula, *yia sou*.

38. ΚΑΛΑΝΤΑ ΤΟΥ ΛΑΖΑΡΟΥ

Χρῆστος Λιαρετίδης
Χ. Κεντρικόν, Κιλκίς

᾽Άγε Λάζαρε, ῞Άγε Δημήτρη,
δές τά σκυλάκια σου νά μή μᾶς φᾶνε.
Καί οἱ κοτοῦλες σου, αὐγά γενᾶνε·
δῶς τα ἐμας καί σας γιά νά τά φᾶμε.

KALANDA FOR LAZARUS DAY

Saint Lazarus, Saint Dhimitri,
tie up your little dogs so they won't eat us up.
And your little hens have laid some eggs—
give them to us and to you, so we can eat them.

39. ΚΑΛΑΝΤΑ ΤΩΝ ΒΑ·Ι·ΩΝ

Μύρων Ἰωαννίδης
Χ. Κεντρικόν, Κιλκίς

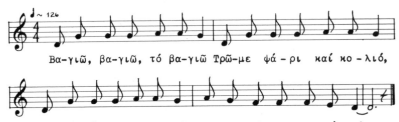

Βα-γι-ῶ, βα-γι-ῶ, τό βα-γι-ῶ Τρῶ–με ψά - ρι καί κο - λιό,

Καί τήν ἄλ-λη Κυ-ρι-α-κή Τρῶ–με κόκ-κι - νο αὐ - γό—

Βαγιῶ, βαγιῶ, τό βαγιῶ,
τρῶμε ψάρι καί κολιό,
καί τήν ἄλλη Κυριακή
τρῶμε κόκκιυο αὐγό.

Θεία, θεία, σύ τό κουλούρι κ᾽ ἐγώ τ᾽ αὐγό.

KALANDA FOR PALM SUNDAY

On Palm Sunday
we eat fish and mackerel,
and next Sunday
we'll eat red eggs.

[Spoken rapidly] :
Aunty, you take the koulouri and I['ll take] the egg.

40. ΚΑΛΑΝΤΑ ΤΩΝ ΧΡΙΣΤΟΥΓΕΝΝΩΝ

Εἰρήνη Καμπουλίδη καί
Θεοδώρα Γιωργάδου
Χ. Κουδούνια, Δράμας

Χρι - στού - γεν - να, πρω - τού - γεν - να, πρω-

τή γιορ - τή τοῦ χρό - - νου.

Χριστούγεννα, πρωτούγεννα, πρωτή γιορτή τοῦ χρόνου.
Γιά βγῆτε, δῆτε, μάθετε πῶς ὁ Χριστός γεννιέται,
γεννιέται κι ἀνατρέφεται μέ μέλι καί μέ γάλα.
Τό μέλι τρῶν' οἱ ἄρχοντες, τό γάλα οἱ παπάδες,
5   καί τό μελισσοβότανο νά λούζονται κυράδες.

Παίψεμα:
Κυρά μ' καλή, κυρά μ' χρυσή, κυρά μ' εὐτυχισμένη,
κυρά μ' μέ τόν υἱγιόκα σου καί μέ τόν πρωτογιόκα σου,
γιά λούσ' τονε, γιά χτένισ' το, γιά στειλ' το στό σχολειὸ·
νά τόν εἰδῆ ὁ δάσκαλος μέ τό χρυσό βιβλίο·
10   νά τόν εἰποῦν τ' ἄλλα παιδιά: ἔλα γιά νά χαροῦμε
καί τίς μεγάλες ἑορτές τά κάλαντα νά ποῦμε.

KALANDA FOR CHRISTMAS

Christ's birth, first birth, first holiday of the year.
Come out and see and learn that Christ is born,
born and bred with honey and with milk.
Nobles eat the honey, priests' wives the milk,
5 and the honeysuckle is for ladies to wash themselves with.

Penema:
Good lady, golden lady, fortunate lady,
lady with your son, your first-born son,
wash him and comb him and send him to school
so the schoolteacher with the golden book can see him,
10 so the other children can say to him: "Come let's be glad
and sing the *kalanda* for the Christmas holidays."

41. ΚΑΛΑΝΤΑ ΤΟΥ ΛΑΖΑΡΟΥ

Εἰρώη Καμπουλίδη καί
Θεοδώρα Γιωργάδου
Χ. Κουδούνια, Δράμας

Λα-ζα-ρός σα-βα-νω-μέ-νος Καί μέ τό κε-ρι ζω-μέ-νος.

Λάζαρος σαβανωμένος
καί μέ τό κερί ζωμένος.

—Πές μας, Λάζαρε, τί εἶδες
εἰς τόν ᾽Αδη ὅπου πῆγες;

5 —Εἶδα φόβους, εἶδα τρόμους,
εἶδα βάσανα καί πόνους.

Δῶστε μου λίγο νεράκι
νά ξεπλύνω τό φαρμάκι

τῆς καρδιᾶς μου, τῶ᾽ χειλέων
10 καί μή μέ ρωτᾶτε πλέον.

Τότε Μάρϑα κ᾽ ἡ Μαρία
ἦσαν ὅλη Βηϑανία.

Δόξα τόν Θεόν φωνάζουν
καί τό Λάζαρο ξετάζουν.

KALANDA FOR LAZARUS DAY

Lazarus, shrouded
and with a candle, but alive.

"Tell us, Lazarus, what did you see
in Hades where you went?"

5   "I saw fears, I saw terrors,
I saw troubles and pains.

Give me a little water
to wash out the poison

from my heart, from my lips,
10   and don't ask me anything more."

Then Martha and Maria
made it known to all of Bethany.

They gave thanks to God
and examined Lazarus.

42. ΤΡΑΓΟΥΔΙ ΤΟΥ ΓΑΜΟΥ

Κυριακή Βλαχοπούλου
Χ. Αὐλή, Καβάλλας

Βαρέθηκα, μπιζεύτισα[1] γιά μιά γειτό-, γιά μιά γειτόνισσά μου.

Κάθε πρωγί στήν πόρτα μου νά μέ ρωτᾶ πού πάγω:
—Πού ἦσ'ναν ἰψ ές, λεβέντη μου, πού ἦσ'ναν ἰψές[2] τό βράδυ;
—Ν-ἰψ ές ν-ἤμουν στή μάνα μου, προξές στήν ἀδελφή μου,

---

[1] Μπιζεύτισα = βαρέθηκα (λ.τ. *bizaret*).
[2] Πρόψες.

5   κι ἀπόψη, μαυρομάτα μου, θά κοιμηθοῦμ᾽ ἀντάμα
    σι πάπλουμα μεταξουτό, σι πουπουλένιο στρῶμα.

Κι ὡς πρέπει τ᾽ ἄσπρο ἄλο᾽[3] σί πράσινα λειβάδια,
Ν-ἔτσι θά πρέπ᾽ κ᾽ ἡ νύφη μας μέ τού γαμπρό σέ ἄσπρα μαξηλάρια.

WEDDING SONG

I'm getting tired of a neighbor girl—
every morning she's at my door, asking me where I'm going.
"Where were you last night, *levendi*, where were you [the night
before]?"
"Last night I was at my mother's; the night before at my sister's;
5   and tonight, black eyes, we'll be sleeping together
under a silken quilt, on a downy mattress."

As the white horse [?] becomes the green valley,
so our bride and groom will become the white pillows.

[3] ᾽Άλογο (;).

43. ΚΑΛΑΝΤΑ ΤΗΣ ΠΡΩΤΟΧΡΟΝΙΑΣ

Κυριακή Βλαχοπούλου
Χ. Αυλή, Καβάλλας

Ἀρχιμηνιά κι ἀρχιχρονιά κι ἀρχή καλο, κι ἀρχή καλός μας χρόνος.

Τ ώρα γεννεθῆ ὁ Χριστός στόν κόσμον πιριπατεῖ,
κ' ἐκεῖ πού πιριπάτιξι βρίσκει τούν ' Ἄη Βασιλη.
—Ν-ώρα καλή σου, Βασιληά, καλό ζιβγάρι κάνεις.
5   —Καλό του λέμ', ἀφέντη μου, καλό καί βλουγημένο.
Ν-όπου τό βλόγησα' ὁ Χριστός μέ τό διξι του χέρι.

Παινέματα:
Πολλά 'παμε κυρ' Βασιληά, ν' ἄς ποῦμε κι τόν γυιόν του:
Τ όν ἔλουσι, τούν χτένισι καί στό σχολειῶ τοῦ στέλνει.
Τ όν ἔβαλω ὁ δάσκαλος γιά νά καλα'χινίση.
10 Καί τοῦ ξιφεύγει τοῦ κίρι κ' ἔκαιγε τό χαρτί του.
Τ όν ἔδειρω ὁ δάσκαλος μέ δυό κλωνιά τοῦ μόσκο.
—Μωρέ, πού εἶν' τά γράμματα, μωρέ, πού εἶν' ὁ νούς σου;
—Τά γράμματα 'νι στό χαρτί κι ὁ νούς μου στίς κοπέλλις·
Δέν εἶναι μόν' στίς ἔμορφες, μόν' εἶν' κ' εἰς μαυρομάτις.

15 Πολλά 'παμε τούν γιούκα του, ν' ἄς ποῦμε κι τῆς κόρης:
Γραμμιτικός τήν προξηνᾶ, μά διάκος τή γυρεύει.
Γυρεύ' ἀμπέλια τρυγητά, ν-ἀμπέλια τρυγημένα·
γυρεύ' χωράφια θεριστά, χωράφια θιρισμένα·
γυρεύει κι τή θάλασσα μί ὅλα τά καράβια·
20 γυρεύει κι τό γερ-βορηᾶ νά τά καλαρμενίση.

Πολλά 'παμι τῆς κόρης της, ἄς ποῦμε κι 'ς βαῖτ σας:
Βαῖτσ' ἄναψ' τό κιρί κι ἀνέβα κι κατέβα.
Φέρι πανέρια κάστανα, πανέρια πορτοκάλλια·
φέρι κι τού γλυκό κρασί νά πιοῦν τά παλληκάρια.

25 Κύτταξι καί τή τσέπη σου κι ὅτ' ἔχεις νά μᾶς δώσης·
ἄν εἶναι γρόσσα, δώσι μας, φλώρια μήν τᾶ λυπᾶσι,
ἄν εἶναι καί μονόγροσα, νά μήν τά λογαριάξεις.

Εἰς ἔτη πολλά καί τοῦ χρόνου εἶσθε καλά.

KALANDA FOR NEW YEAR'S

The month's beginning, the year's beginning, and the beginning of a
good year for us.
Now Christ is born and walks on earth,
and, there where he's walking, he meets Saint Vasili.
"Good hour to you, Vasilia, that's a fine team you've got there."
5 "We call it fine [?], *afendi*, fine and blessed."
Whereupon Christ blessed it with his right hand.

Penemata:
We've said a lot about Mr. Vasilia, let's talk about his son now:
He washed him and combed him and sent him to school.
The teacher set him to make a good beginning,
10 but he dropped his candle and it burned his paper.
The teacher beat him with two musk branches.
"Where are your letters, child? Where is your mind?"
"The letters are on the paper and my mind is on the girls,
and not only on beautiful ones but on black-eyed ones, too."

15 We've said a lot about his son, let's talk about his daughter:
A clerk has sent his marriage consul, a deacon has asked for her hand.
As a dowry, he's asking for vineyards full of grapes
and harvested fields
and the sea with all its ships
20 and old Northwind to sail them well.

We've said a lot about his daughter, let's talk about the maid:
Maid, light the candle and go up and down,
bring baskets of chestnuts, baskets of oranges,
and bring out some sweet wine so the *pallikaria* can drink.

25 Look in your pocket and give us whatever you've got—
if it's *grosa*, give them to us; if it's florins, don't be sorry
    to see them go;
and if it's *monogrosa*, don't even count them.

44. Η ΠΡΟΣΦΥΓΟΔΛΑ

Ελένη Τιτιγιάννη
Χ. Παναγία, Θάσου

Αρ-χον - - το-γιό, άρ-χον - το -
γιός παν-τρευ - ι - ται__ Κι __ παίρ - νει
Προσ-φυ-γού-λα,__ Προσ-φυ-γού-λα, μαυ-ρο-μα - τα
μου__ Κι __ παίρ - - νει Προσ-φυ-γού-λα,__
Προσ-φυ - γού - λα, σέ κλαῖν τά μά - τια μου.

Ἀρχοντογιό', ἀρχοντογιός παντρεύεται
    κι παίρνει Προσφυγούλα, Προσφυγούλα, μαυρομάτα μου,
    κι παίρνει Προσφυγούλα, Προσφυγούλα, σέ κλαίν' τά μάτια μου.

Βρέ ἡ μάνα του σάν τ' ἄκουσε, πέφτει, λιγοθυμάει.
Πιάνει δυό φίδια ζωντανά, παίρνει τά τηγανίζει.
— Ἔλα νύφη νά φᾶς φαγί, ψάρια τηγανισμένα.
5 Καί μέ τήν πρώτη πηρουνιά, καρδιά της φαρμακώθει.
— Τώρα, κυρ' πιθιρά, νερό, τώρα ψυχή μου βγαίνει.
— Ἀλάργα νύφη μ', τό νερό, ἀλάργα τό πηγάδι.

PROSFIGHOULA

The noble's son married and took for a wife Prosfighoula.
His mother, soon as she heard about it, fell into a faint.
She took two live snakes, took them and fried them.
"Come, daughter-in-law, come and eat fried fish."
5 And, with the first forkful, her heart was poisoned.
"Water, now, mother-in-law, my soul is leaving me."
"Too far away the water, daughter-in-law, too far away the well."

Tsakisma:
My black-eyed Prosfighoula,
Prosfighoula, my eyes are crying for you.

45. ΘΕΛΩ ΝΑ ΠΑΩ ΣΤΗΝ ΑΡΑΠΙΑ

'Ελένη Τιτιγιάννη
Χ. Παναγία, Θάσου

θέ - λω _____ νά πά-, θέ - λω νά

πά-γω στήν 'Α - - ρα - πιά Νά κλέψ' ἔν' 'Α - ρα-

πά - κι, νά κλέψ' ἔν' 'Α - ρα - πά - κι,

Θέλω νά πά-, θέλω νά πάγω στήν 'Αραπιά
νά κλέψ' ἔν' 'Αραπάκι, νά κλέψ' ἔν' 'Αραπάκι,
νά κάθωμαι, νά κάθωμαι νά τό ρωτῶ,
πῶς πιάνεται ἡ ἀγάπη, πῶς πιάνεται ἡ ἀγάπη.

'Από τά μά-, ἀπό τά μάτια πιάνεται·
στ' ἀχειλη κατεβαίνει, ριζώνει καί δέν βγαίνει·
ἀπό τ' ἀχεί-, ἀπό τ' ἀχειλη στήν καρδιά,
ριζώνει καί δέν βγαίνει, μικρή μου χαϊδεμένη.

I WANT TO GO TO ARAPIA

I want to go to Arapia to steal an *Arapaki*,
to sit down and ask him how love is caught.

It's caught from the eyes, it goes down to the lips;
from the lips to the heart, it takes root and never comes out.

46. ΧΕΛΙΔΟΝΙΣΜΑ

Ἑλένη Τιτιγιάννη
Χ. Παναγία, Θάσου

Μάρτη, Μάρτη βρόχερε καί Φλεβάρης χιόνερε,
ὁ 'πριλης ὁ γλυκύς ἦρθε σήμερ' δ έν εὦ' μακρύς.
Τά πουλάκια κελαιδοῦν, τά δεντράκια φυλλανθοῦν,
τά 'ορνίθια ἀρχινοῦν νά γέννουν καί νά κλῶσσουν.
5 Τά κατσίκια ἀρχινοῦν ν' ἀνεβαίνουν στά κλαριά·
τά κοπάδια ἀρχινοῦν καί νά τρώγουν τά κλαριά.[1]
Ζῶα, ἄνθρωποι, πουλί χαίρεσθ' ἀπό καρδιά.

[1] Οἱ στίχοι 5-6 εἶναι ἀνακατωμένοι· σωστά εἶναι:
Τά κοπάδια ἀρχινοῦν νά ἀνεβαίνουν στά βουνά,
τά κατσίκια ἀρχινοῦν καί νά τρώγουν τά κλαριά.
(Βλ. Passow, 225-226.)

KHELIDHONISMA

March, rainy March, and snowy February,
and sweet April isn't far off.
Little birds sing, little trees leaf out,
hens start to lay eggs and set.
5   [Flocks start to go up to the mountains,
nanny goats start eating branches.]
Animals, men, birds, be glad in your hearts.

47. ΠΡΟΣΚΥΝΗ ΤΟΥ ΤΡΑΠΕΖΟΥ ΤΗΣ ΠΡΩΤΟΧΡΟΝΙΑΣ

'Αργύρη Κουτούπη Τσόγγου
Χ. Λιμένα, Θάσου

' Άγιου Βασιλη, πού τραγουδοῦν τά χειλη, κάνετε προσκυνή μας:
' Άγιου Βασιλη, πού τραγουδοῦν τά χειλη,
ἔλα πού σέ περιμένουν τά καλά παιδιά.
Μέσα στήν σακκούλα θά τά φέρης οὖλα:
μῆλα καί σταφιδες, κούκλες, πιγνιδάκια καί πολλές εὐχές.
5   [Τά ἄσπρα σου τά γένεια πού μοιάζουν τ' ἀσιμένια.]
Φόρεσε τή κάπα, 'κεῖνη παγωνιά,
κ'ἔλα μέ τά δώρα, μέ καλή χρονιά.

TABLE GRACE FOR NEW YEAR'S EVE

Saint Vasili, whom the lips are singing about, say grace:

Saint Vasili, whom the lips are singing about,
come, because the good children are waiting for you.
You're going to bring everything in your sack:
apples, raisins, dolls, games, and many good wishes.
5   [Your white beard looks like silver.]
Wear your frosty cap
and come with the gifts, with the good year.

OI ΣΠΟΡΑΔΕΣ

SPORADES ISLANDS

48. ΤΡΑΓΟΥΔΙ ΤΟΥ ΓΑΜΟΥ

Εὐφροσύνη Τσακαμῆ
Σκῦρος

Δυό ἥ - λιοι, δυό _____ φεγ - γά - ρε - α, _____

Δυό ἥ - λιοι, δυ - ό _____ φεγ - γά - ρια __

Δυό __ ἥ - λιοι, δυό φεγ - γά - ρε - α Βγή - κα - νε

σή - - με - ρα, βγή - κα - νε σή - - με - ραϡ -

Δυό ἥλιοι, δυό φεγγάρια (τρίς)
  βγήκανε σήμερα, βγήκανε σήμερα,
Τ᾿ ὦνα στό πρόσωπό σου, (τρίς)
  τ᾿ ἄλλο στά σύνεφα, ἀμάν ἀμάν.

WEDDING SONG

Two suns, two moons came out today:
the one in your face, the other in the clouds.

49. ΤΟ ΚΑΠΕΛΙΚΟ[1] (*Τοῦ τραπεζοῦ τοῦ γάμου*)

Εὐφροσύνη Τσακαμῆ
Σκῦρος

Δέν εἶ - μαι ψε-, λέϊ, δέν εἶ - - -

μαι ____ ψεύ - τι - κος πα - - - ρᾶς

Νά, _____ αχ, ___ νά μέ πε - τά -

ξης ___ πέ - - - - - ρα,

Μπρέ μπρέ μπρέ ___ μπρέ μπρέ μπρέ ___ μπε-ρέ,

Νά, _____ αχ, νά μέ πε - τά-

ξης ___ πέ - - - - ρα, ἄχ,

[1] Καπέλλος = τσοπάνης καί χωριάτης.

Μα - ζύ __ σου πα - - ντα νᾶ - μου - - - νε.

Δέν εἶμαι ψε-, λέϊ, δ έν εἶμαι ψεύτικος παρᾶς
να, ἄχ, νά μέ πετάξης πέρα, μπρέ, μπρέ, μπρέ, μπρέ, μπρέ, μπρέ,
να, ἄχ, νά μέ πετάξης πέρα, ἄχ, μαξύ σου πάντα νάμουνα.
Εἶμαι βενέ-, βάϊ, εἶμαι βενέτικο φλουρί
μέσ' ἀπ' τήν ταμπακέρα, ἀμάν, ἀμάν, ἀμάν,
μέσ' ἀπ' τήν ταμπακέρα, ἄχ, ἀμάν, σεβδί, 'μάν, 'μάν.

SHEPHERD'S SONG (Wedding table song)

I'm no false coin, that you can throw me away—
I'm a Venetian florin inside the cigarette case.

50. ΤΡΑΓΟΥΔΙ ΤΟΥ ΓΑΜΟΥ (Τῆς τάβλας)

Εὐφροσύνη Τσακαμή
Σκῦρος

Βρα - δυά - ζει καί _____ πα - ρα - κα - λῶ,

Πό - τε νά ξη - με - ρώ - ση; ῎Ε - λιμ για -

λέ - λιμ ῎ε - λιμ γιά-λέ - λιμ ῎ε - λιμ γιά-_____

Πό - τε νά ξη - με - ρώ - ση; Πάρ' τό μα -

χαῖ - ρι, πάρ' τό μα-χαῖ - ρι δῶς μου μιά.

Γύρισμα

῎Ε - λα νά πᾶ - - με ῎Α - γου-λα _____,
Νά σέ φι - λῶ _____ στά μά - γου-λα _____.

Βραδυάζει καί παρακαλῶ, (δίς)
πότε νά ξημερώση; ἔλιμ γιαλέλιμ, ἔλιμ γιαλέλιμ, ἔλιμ για-,
πότε νά ξημερώση; πάρ' τό μαχαῖρι, πάρ' τό μαχαῖρι, δῶς μου μιά.
Γιά νά σέ δοῦν, μαυραμάτα μου,
γιά νά σέ δοῦν, σέ δοῦν τά μάτια μου
κι ὁ νοῦς μου νά μερώση, ἔλιμ γιαλέλιμ, ἔλιμ γιαλέλιμ, ἔλιμ για-,
κι ὁ νοῦς μου νά μερώση, καϋμό καί λαῦρα, καϋμό καί λαῦρα
πέρασα.

Γύρισμα:
Ἔλα νά πᾶμε, Ἀγουλα,
νά σέ φιλῶ στά μάγουλα.
Νά σέ φιλῶ στά μάγουλα,
ἔλα νά πᾶμε, Ἀγουλα.

WEDDING SONG (Table song)

Evening is falling and I ask, when will day break?
So my eyes can see you and my mind be tamed.

Yirisma:
Come, let's go, Aghoula,
so I can kiss you on the cheeks.

51. ΣΤΟΝ ΚΑΛΕ[1] (Τοῦ γάμου)

Εὐφροσύνη Τσακαμῆ
Σκῦρος

Μα - ρέ γιέ, μα - ρέ γιέ, Μα - ρέ γιέ μου
κα - να - - κά - ρι, μα - ρέ γιέ
Μα - ρέ γιέ μου κα - να - κα - ρι, Ποιά γυ - ναῖτ - κα
θά σέ πά - ρη, ποιά γυ - ναῖτ -

Μαρέ[2] γιέ, μάρέ γιέ,
μαρέ γιέ μου κανακάρι, μαρέ γιέ,
μαρέ γιέ μου κανακάρι,
ποιά γυναῖκα θά σέ πάρη; ποιά γυναι-

[1] Στό καλό.
[2] Μωρέ.

Ποιά κυρά καί ποιά κοκκώνα[3]
θά σοῦ στρώνη τά σεντόνια;

5 Μαρέ γιέ μου, ποῦσουνε
κι ὅλοι μ᾽ ἀρωτοῦσανε;

᾽Ημουνα στό πανηγύρι
μ᾽ ἕνα ξένο νοικοκύρη.

STON KALE (Wedding dance song)

"My son, my little darling,
which woman is going to marry you?

Which lady, which fine lady
is going to lay out the sheets for you?

5 My son, where were you
when everyone was asking for you?"

"I was at the festival
with a foreign gentleman."

[3] Κοκκώνα = κυρία.

52. ΤΡΑΓΟΥΔΙ ΤΩΝ ΑΠΟΚΡΕΩΝ

Εὐφροσύνη Τσακαμή
Σκῦρος

Τί νά τοῦ κα - νω τοῦ _____ και -

ρου _____ τοῦ _____ χρό-, τοῦ χρό - νου

τοῦ _____ κα-, τοῦ _____

χρό - νου τοῦ καϋ - μέ - - - - νου

Πού μοῦ - κα - νε τήν δ - ψη _____ μου ὁ - σά', _____ ὁ-

σάν _____ τοῦ _____ πε - - - - - θα -, _____

ὁ - σάν τοῦ _____ πε - θα - μέ - - - - - νου.

Βά - λε - τε μου σί - - δε - ρα _____ βα - ρε -

γιά   γιατ' ἔ-, _____ γιατ' ἔ - χω _____

πό - - - - - νο _____ γιατ' ἔ -

χω ____ πό - νο ____ στήν, ____ βρέ, στήν καρ - δι - ά.

Τί νά τοῦ κάνω τοῦ καιροῦ τοῦ χρό-, τοῦ χρόνου τοῦ κα-, τοῦ χρόνου
τοῦ καϋμένου
πού μοὔκανε τήν ὄψη μου ὀσάν, ὀσάν τοῦ πεθα-, ὀσάν τοῦ πεθαμένου.

Βάλετέ μου σίδερα βαρειά
γιατ' ἔχω, γιατ' ἔχω πόνο, γιατ' ἔχω πόνο στήν, βρέ, στήν καρδιά.

SONG FOR CARNIVAL

What can I do with this time of year
that makes my face like that of a dead man?

Put me in heavy irons
for I've got pain in my heart.

53. ΤΡΑΓΟΥΔΙ ΤΗΣ ΚΑΘΑΡΑΣ ΔΕΥΤΕΡΑΣ

Εὐφροσύνη Τσακαμῆ
Σκῦρος

"Αν καί _____ τό χέ-, βάϊ-νον, ἄν καί τό___

χέ - ρι σου _____ κτυ - πᾶς, τό χέ - ρι

σου_ κτυ - πᾶς _____ τόν _ ἀ-, τόν ἀ - δακ -

τύ - - - - λι', _____ τόν_ ἀ -

δακ - τύ - λι' μό - - - νο,

"Ωχ, _____ ὅ - λο τό σῶ - μα τό _ γρι -

κᾶ τό _____ βά-, _____ τό βά - ρο_

σκέ - - - το, ——————— βά -

ρο— σκέ - τον— πό - - - νο

"Ε - λα νά κου - βεν - τιά - σω - με Γιά—

νά, —— γιά νά —— μᾶς—— δοῦν ———————

νά, ———— γιά — νά μᾶς — δοῦν———

νά — σκά-, ἄχ, νά σκά - σου - νε.

' Ἂν καί τό χέ-, βάϊνον, ἂν καί τό χέρι σου κτυπᾶς, τό χέρι σου κτυπᾶς
τόν ἀ-, τόν ἀδακτύλι', τόν ἀδακτύλι' μόνο,
ὤχ, ὅλο τό σῶμα τό γρικᾶ[1] τό βά-, τό βάρο σκέτο, βάρο σκέτο πόνο.

' Ἔλα νά κουβεντιάσωμε
γιά νά μᾶς δοῦν νά σκά-, ἄχ, νά σκάσουνε.

[1] Γρικᾶ = ἀκούει.

SONG FOR CLEAN MONDAY

Although you strike only your ringless hand,
ah, the whole body hears the heavy dull pain.

Come, let's talk together,
so they can see us and hush.

54. ΤΡΑΓΟΥΔΙ ΤΗΣ ΠΡΩΤΟΜΑΓΙΑΣ

Εὐφροσύνη Τσακαμῆ
Σκῦρος

Τό   Μά - η   ἐ - - - - γεν - - - -

νή - - - - - θη - κα   Καί _____

μά - - για _____ δέν _____

φο - , _____ ἄχ,   καί   μά - -

για _____ καί _____ μά - -

για _____ δέν _____

φο - - - - βοῦ - - μαι,

Μά - η μου μέ τά _____
Μέ χα - ρές καί μέ _____

λου - - - λού - δι - α _____
τρα - - - γού - - δι - α.

Τό Μάη ἐγεννήϑηκα καί μάγια δέ φο-, ὤχ, καί μάγια, καί μάγια δέ
φοβοῦμαι,
ἐξόν ἄν μέ μαγέψουνε στήν κλίνη ὁπού κοι-, στήν κλίνη ὁ-, στήν κλίνη
ὁπού κοιμοῦμαι.

Μάη μου μέ τά λουλούδια,
μέ χαρές καί μέ τραγούδια.

SONG FOR MAY DAY

I was born in May and I fear no witchcraft,
except if they bewitch me in my bed where I sleep.

May with the flowers,
with joys and songs.

55. Ο ΑΥΛΟΝΙΤΙΑΤΙΚΟΣ

Εὐφροσύνη Τσακαμῆ
Σκῦρος

Δέν - τρι μου βερ - γο - λυ - γε - ρή

καί δάφ - νη τοῦ δαφ - νῶ — — να

Κι ἀ-γά - πη κα — — λο - και - ρι - νή,

νά σ' εἶ - χα τό__ χει - μώ — — — να,

Κι ἀ-γά - πη κα — — — λο - και - ρι - νή

νά σ' εἶ - χα τό__ χει - μώ — — — να__

Δέν - τρι μου βερ — — γο — λυ — — γε - ρή

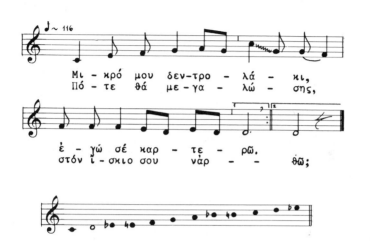

Δέντρι μου βεργολυγερή καί δάφνη τοῦ δαφνῶνα
κι ἀγάπη καλοκαιρινή, νά σ'εἶχα τό χειμώνα. (δίς)
Δέντρι μου βεργολυγερή καί δάφνη τοῦ δαφνῶνα.

Γύρισμα:
Μικρό μου δεντρολάκι, ἐγώ σέ καρτερῶ.
Πότε θά μεγαλώσης, στόν ἴσκιο σου νὰρθῶ;

RAVINE SONG

Tree, willowy switch, laurel of the laurel grove,
summer love, I wish I had you in the wintertime.

Yirisma:
Little tree, I'm waiting for you—
when are you going to get big so I can come to your shade?

56. ΣΤΗΝ ΑΓΙΑ ΠΑΡΑΣΚΕΥΗ

Παρασκευή Σοφοκήτου μέ
χορωδία κοριτσιών
Σκόπελος

Μέσ᾽ στήν, μανούλα μου, μέσ᾽ στήν Ἁγία Παρασκευή,
μέσ᾽ στήν Ἁγία Παρασκευή
κοιμᾶται κόρη μοναχή.

Κοιμᾶται κι ὀνειρεύεται
καὶ βλέπει πῶς παντρεύεται.

5 Βλέπ᾽ ἔνα πύργον ἐψηλό
καὶ δυό ποτάμια μέ νερό.

—Ὁ πύργος εἰν᾽ ὁ ἄντρας μου,
τό περιβόλι ὁ γάμος μου,

τά δυό ποτάμια μέ νερό,
10 κρασί γιά τά συμπεθεριό.

—Ὁ πύ-, *κορούλα μου*, ὁ πύργος εἰν᾽ ὁ χάρος σου,
ὁ πύργος εἰν᾽ ὁ χάρος σου,
τό περιβόλι ὁ τάφος σου,

τά δυό ποτάμια μέ νερό,
τά δάκρυα πού θά χύνω ἐγώ.

AT THE CHAPEL OF SAINT PARASKEVI

At the chapel of Saint Paraskevi
a girl is sleeping all alone.

She sleeps and she dreams
and she sees that she is being married.

5 She sees a tall tower
and two rivers with water.

"Mother, the tower is my husband,
the orchard my wedding,

and the two rivers with water
10 wine for the in-laws."

"Daughter, the tower is your death,
the orchard your grave,

and the two rivers with water
the tears that I'll shed."

57. Η ΟΡΦΑΝΗ

Παρασκευή Σοφοκήτου μέ
χορωδία κοριτσιῶν
Σκόπελος

Μιά μά-, κα - λέ, μιά μά - να εἶ - χε ἔ - μορ-
φη, Μιά μά-, κα - λέ, μιά μά - να
εἶ - χε ἔ - μορ - φη, Μιά μά - να εἶ - χε
ἔ - μορ-φη,____ μιά ἀ-κρι-βο- θυ - γα - τέ- ρα, Μιά   τέ - ρα.

Μιά μά-, καλέ, μιά μάνα εἶχε ἔμορφη, (δίς)
μιά μάνα εἶχε ἔμορφη, μιά ἀκριβοθυγατέρα.

Τήν ἔλουζε, τήν κτένιζε μέ διαμαντένια κτένια.
Ἦλθε ὁ καιρός καί πέθανε, ἡ μάνα τῆς καϋμένης.
Πολύς καιρός δέν πέρασ' ὁ πατέρας της παντρεύθη.
5 Παίρνει γυναῖκα μιάν ὀχιά, τήν ἔβαλε νά γνέθη·

τῆς κόβει τά σγουρά μαλλιά, τῆς κεφάλης στολίδια,
τῆς βγάζει ἀπό τά δάχτυλα τἄμορφα δαχτυλίδια.
—Ἐσύ 'σαι κόρη ὀρφανή, κόρη ὀρφανεμένη,
πρέπει νά πᾶς στό μαγειριό καί δοῦλα μας νά γένης.
10 Τήν πιάνει τό παράπονο καί στό κοιμ᾿τῆρι πάει.
—Σήκω μανοῦλα κι ἄκουσε, σήκω καί ἄκουσέ με,
ξένη μανοῦλα ἔκανα καί παρηγόρησέ με.
καί ξένες ἔκαν᾿ ἀδελφές καί ξένοι μέ φωνάζουν
μέ δέρνουν, μέ σκοτώνουνε, μέσ᾿ στήν καρδιά μέ σφάζουν.

THE ORPHAN

A mother had a beautiful, precious daughter—
she washed her and combed her hair with a diamond comb.
The time came, and the unfortunate girl's mother died.
Soon afterward her father remarried.
5 He took a woman, a viper, who set her to spin.
She cut off her curly hair, the ornament of her head;
she took her beautiful rings from her fingers.
"You're an orphan, an orphan girl,
you must go to the kitchen and become our servant."
10 She took her grievances and went to the cemetery.
"Rise up, mother, and listen, rise up and hear me—
I've got a stranger for a mother, console me,
I've got strangers for sisters, and strangers order me about.
They beat me, they kill me, they tear me in my heart."

58. ΜΠΑΙΝΩ Σ'ΑΔΕΙΟ ΠΕΡΙΒΟΛΙ

Σταματία Καλιμάνη μέ
χορωδία κοριτσιῶν
Σκόπελος

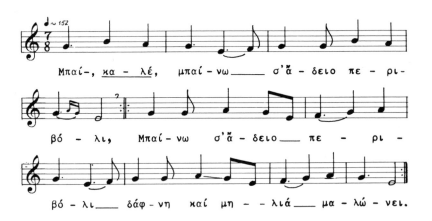

Μπαί-, καλέ, μπαίνω σ' ἄδεισ περιβόλι,
μπαίνω σ' ἄδειο περιβόλι,
δάφνη καί μηλιά μαλώνει.

Δάφνη, μοῦκοψες κλωνάρι,
θά σέ πάρη τό ποτάμι.

5   Θά σέ πάη δύσι-δύσι
κάτω στοῦ πασᾶ τή βρύση.

'Κεῖ πού πλέναν κι ἀπ-ἀπλώναν
οἱ μελάχροινες τά ροῦχα,

τά πλυμένα διπλωμένα
10 καί στήν πλάκα πλακωμένα.

Κι ἀπό κατ᾽ ἀπό τήν πλάκα
κάθεται μιά μαυραμάτα,

κ᾽ἔπλεγε χρυσό γαϊτάνι
καί χρυσό μαργαριτάρι.

I GO INTO AN EMPTY ORCHARD

I go into an empty orchard—
laurel and apple tree are quarreling:

Laurel, you cut down my branch;
the river will take you away.

5 It will carry you westward,
down to the pasha's spring,

where the brown-haired girls
are washing and drying their clothes;

the washed clothes, the folded clothes,
10 flattened on a rock,

and beneath the rock
sits a black-eyed girl

making a gold braid
and a gold pearl.

59. ΣΤΟΝ ΑΔΗ ΘΑ ΚΑΤΕΒΩ

Σταματία Καλιμάνη μέ
χορωδία κοριτσιῶν
Σκόπελος

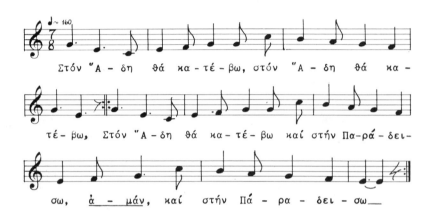

Στόν ῞Αδη ϑά κατέβω (τρίς)
    καί στήν Παράδεισο, ἀμάν, καί στήν Παράδεισο,
τό Χάρο ν᾽ ἀνταμώσω (τρίς)
    δυό λόγια νά τοῦ εἰπῶ, ἀμάν, δυό λόγια νά τοῦ εἰπῶ.

Χάρε, γιά χάρισέ μου σαΐτες κοφτερές
νά πάω νά σαϊτέψω δυό τρεῖς μελαχροινές,

5 ποῦχουν στά χειλη βάμμα, στό μάγουλο ἐληά,
   κι ἀνάμεσα στά στήϑη χρυσή πορτοκαλλιά.

Κάνει τά πορτοκάλλια καί δέν μυρίζουνε,
νά τρών᾽ τά παλληκάρια νά δαιμονίζωνται.

I'M GOING DOWN TO HADES

I'm going down to Hades and to Paradise
to meet with Charon and have a couple of words with him:

Charon, come give me some sharp arrows
so I can go out and shoot two or three dark-haired girls

5   who have paint on their lips and beauty marks on their cheeks,
and between their breasts a golden orange tree.

It makes oranges with no odor,
so the *pallikaria* can eat and get devilish.

60. ΚΥΝΗΓΟΣ ΠΟΥ ΚΥΝΗΓΟΥΣΕ

Κατίνα Βλαχάκη μέ
χορωδία κοριτσιῶν
Σκόπελος

Χέ, κυνηγός, κυνηγός, κυνηγός πού κυνηγοῦσε, (δίς)
χέ, κυνηγός πού κυνηγοῦσε
μέσ᾽ στά δάση τριγυρνοῦσε,

μέσ᾽ στά ὄρη, στά βουνά,
κυνηγώντας τά πουλιά.

5 Ξαφνά βλέπ᾽ ἕνα πουλί
νά πετάη σέ κλαρί

ἀπό δέντρο σέ κλωνάρι,
ὅλο ἐμορφιά καί χάρη.

Κι ἄρχισε νά κελαϊδῆ,
10 μέ τί πικρά νά μιλῆ:

—Κυνηγέ μου κυνηγάρη,
κάνε μου καί με μιά χάρη.

Ρίξε βόλια στό κορμί μου,
δέν τή θέλω τή ζωή μου.

15 Ν᾽ ἀνεβῶ στούς οὐρανούς
ν᾽ ἀγκαλιάσω τούς νεκρούς.

THE HUNTER WAS HUNTING

The hunter was hunting,
walking around in the forest,

on the mountains,
hunting birds.

5 Suddenly he saw a bird
fly to a branch,

from tree to bough,
all beauty and charm.

And it began to sing—
10 how bitterly it spoke:

"Friend hunter,
do me a favor—

throw a bullet into my body,
I don't want my life.

15 Let me go up to the heavens
and embrace the dead."

61. ΕΝΑΣ ΜΕΓΑΛΟΣ ΒΑΣΙΛΕΑΣ

Μιχαήλ Βλαχάκης μέ
χορωδία
Σκόπελος

' Ε, βασι-, λέϊ, βασιλοπούλα κάθηται,
βασιλοπούλα κάθηται σ' ένα ψηλό παλάτι,
ν-έχει ρηγμένα τά μαλλιά στήν ἀσημένια πλάτη.

Ν-έχει τά λουλούδα τῆς γῆς, τά λουλούδα τοῦ Μάη.
Τό κύρη της περικαλεῖ καί τόν παρακαλάει:

5 —Τί ἔχεις βασιλεά μου κι ὅλου κακουκαρδίζεις;
   Εἶσαι τῆς χώρης καί χωριά κι ὅλη τή γῆν ὁρίζεις.

   —Ν-ἕνας μεγάλος βασιλεᾶς, τό πρῶτο παλληκάρι,
   στρατόν ἔχει ἀμέτρητο, γυρεύει νά μέ πάρη.

   —Γι᾽ αὐτό, κυρέ μου, δέν τό λές, ἐμέ δέν ἐψυχραίνεις·
10 ν-ἐγώ θά πάγω γιά τά σέ καί ν-ἥσυχος νά μένης.

   Καί δῶσε μον σαράντα νιούς, σαράντα παλληκάρια,
   κι ὅλοι ντυμένοι ἤτανε¹ μέσ᾽ στά μαργαριτάρια.

   Νά μπῶ σέ θάλασσα πλατειά, πέλαγος ν᾽ ἀρμενίσω,
   νά πά᾽ νά βρῶ τό βασιλεά νά τόν ἐπολεμήσω.

15 Μέρης πολλές δέν πέρασαν καί ν-ἡ φρηγάδα μπαίνει
   μέσ᾽ ἕν᾽ ὁλόχρυσο λιμάν᾽ κι ὅλου καμαρωμένη,

   μέ ἔμορφους σαράντα νιούς, σαράντα παλληκάρια
   κι ὅλοι ντυμένοι ἤτανε μέσ᾽ στά μαργαριτάρια.

   Νά, ᾽κεῖνη κόρην πρόβαλε σάν ἥλιο, σάν φηγγάρι·
20 λιγουθυμάει μιά καί δυό τ᾽ ὅμορφο παλληκάρι.

   —Ν-ἐγώ δέν κάνω τό γιατρό καί δέν πωλῶ βοτάνι·
   ἔλα νά σέ στεφανωθῶ, ν-ὁ πόνος σου νά γιάνη.

A GREAT KING

A princess sits in a high palace,
her hair falling down her silver back.

She holds flowers of the earth, flowers of May.
She asks her lord, she begs him:

5 "What's wrong, my king, you're so distressed?
   You're the king of the countryside and the villages, you rule all the
   earth."

   "A great king, a chief *pallikari*,
   has an immeasurable army, and he's coming to conquer me."

¹ Νάτανε.

"Don't mention it, my lord, it doesn't scare me at all—
10 I'll go in your place and you won't have to worry.

Give me forty young men, forty *pallikaria*,
and all of them dressed in pearl.

I'll go out onto the broad sea, I'll sail the ocean,
I'll go and find the king and make war on him."

15 Not many days had passed when a frigate
with a proud air enters a golden harbor,

with forty handsome young men, forty *pallikaria*,
and all of them dressed in pearl.

There, the girl appeared, like the sun, like the moon—
20 the handsome *pallikari* faints, one-two-three.

"I'm no doctor and I don't sell medicine—
come, let me marry you and your pain will be cured."

62. ΜΑΝΑ Μ', ΣΤΟ ΠΕΡΙΒΟΛΙ ΜΑΣ

Κερετσούλα Καραγγιόζη μέ
χορωδία
Σκόπελος

Μάνα μ', καλέ μου, μάνα μ', στό περιβόλι μας,
μάνα μ', στό περιβόλι μας καί στή μοσκομηλιά μας, καί στή
μοσκομηλιά μας
τρεῖς ἀ-, καλέ μου μάνα μ', τρεῖς ἀητοί, μανούλα μου,
τρεῖς ἀητοί, μανούλα μου, ἦλθαν στή γειτονιά μας, ἦλθαν στή
γειτονιά μας.

Ν-ὸ ἔ-, καλέ μου, ν-ὸ ἕνας μῆλο μοὔδωσε,
ν-ὸ ἕνας μῆλο μοὔδωσε κι ὁ ἄλλος δακτυλίδι, κι ὁ ἄλλος δακτυλίδι,
κι ὁ τρί-, καλέ μου, κι ὁ τρίτος ὁ μικρότερος,
κι ὁ τρίτος ὁ μικρότερος μέ φίλησε στά χείλη, μέ φίλησε στά χείλη.

5 Τό μῆλο, μάνα μ', τὄραγα, δέν μοὔμενε ψιβγάδι·
μά 'κεῖνος πού μέ φίλησε, μοῦ ἄφισε σημάδι.

—Τό μῆλο ὅπου ἔφαγες εἶν' τῆς χαρᾶς ὁ λόγος,
τό δακτυλίδι, κόρη μο', ὁ φητεινός ὁ χρόνος.

Κ'ἐκεῖνος πού σέ φίλησε καί σ' ἄφησε σημάδι
10 εἶναι ὁ νιός πού σ' ἀγαπᾶ καί ταίρι θά σέ κάνη.

MOTHER, IN OUR ORCHARD

"Mother, in our orchard, at our musk-apple tree,
three eagles came to our neighborhood.

One gave me an apple, and the other a ring,
and the third one, the littlest one, kissed me on the lips.

5 I ate the apple, mother, not a bit was left,
but the one who kissed me left a mark."

"The apple that you ate stands for the wedding,
the ring, daughter, means this year,

and the one who kissed you and left a mark
10 is the youth who loves you and who's going to make you his mate."

63. Ο ΛΕΙΒΑΔΙ ΕΙΝΑΙ ΑΝΘΙΣΜΕΝΟ

Κερετσούλα Καραγγιόζη μέ
χορωδία
Σκόπελος

Ν-ὸ λειβά-, βρέ, ν-ὸ λειβά-, ν-ὸ λειβάδ᾽ εἶν᾽ ἀνθισμένο,
ν-ὸ λειβάδ᾽ εἶν᾽ ἀνθισμένο κι ἀπό λουλούδα σπαρμένο.
᾽Ένα λου-, ἕνα λου-, ἕνα λουλουδάκι βρῆκα,
ἕνα λουλουδάκι βρῆκα, νά τό κόψω δέν μ᾽ ἀφήκαν.

5   ᾽Άσπρο μέ, βρέ, ν-ἄσπρο μέ, ἄσπρο μέ κλαδιά γαλάζα,
ἄσπρο μέ κλαδιά γαλάζα, ν-ὅλο σκέρτσα κι ὅλο νάζα.

Τὄκοψα, νά ζήσωμε παιδιά, τὄκοψα μά ἦταν ἕνα,
τὄκοψα μά ἦταν ἕνα, ἦταν ἕνα σάν καί σένα.

Τὄκοψα, νά ζήσωμε παιδιά, τὄκοψα καί τό μαδοῦσα,
10   τὄκοψα καί τό μαδοῦσα· "μ᾽ ἀγαπᾶς;" τό ἐρωτοῦσα.

"Ναί," ἐκεῖ-, βρέ, "ναί" ἐκεῖ-, "ναί," ἐκεῖνο μ᾽ ἀπαντοῦσε,
"ναί," ἐκεῖνο μ᾽ ἀπαντοῦσε κ᾽ ἔσκυφτε καί μέ φιλοῦσε.

Τότε μά-, νά ζήσωμε παιδιά, τότε μάζεψα τά φύλλα,
τότε μάζαψα τά φύλλα ἕνα-ἕνα καί τά πῆρα

15   νά τά κά-, βρέ, νά τά κά-, νά τά κάνω φυλακτάρι,
νά τά κάνω φυλακτάρι, τή ζωή μο᾽ νά φυλάει.

THE VALLEY'S ALL IN BLOSSOM

The valley's all in blossom
and sown with flowers.

I found a little flower,
but I wasn't allowed to cut it.

5 It was white with blue branches,
all-jesting, all airs and graces.

I cut it,
and it was just like you.

I cut it and I plucked it
10 and I asked it, "Do you love me?"

"Yes," it answered me,
and it bent over and kissed me.

Then I gathered up the leaves
one by one and took them

15 to make them into a prison
to guard my life.

64. ΠΑΛΙ Θ᾽ΑΡΧΙΣΩ ΓΙΑ ΝΑ ΠΩ (Τῆς ξενητειᾶς)

Κερετσούλα Καραγγιόζη μέ
χορωδία
Σκόπελος

"Ε, Πά - λι θ᾽ἀρ-χί - σω _____ γιά νά πῶ
Γιά τῆς ἀ - γά - πης ___ τόν καϋ-μό, Γιά _____ τῆς
ξε-, _____ τῆς ξε - νι - τιᾶς τά μέ - ροι
πού εἶ - ναι τό, πού εἶ - ναι τό δι - κό μου ταῖ - ρι.

''Ε, πάλι θ᾽ ἀρχίσω γιά νά πῶ
γιά τῆς ἀγάπης τόν καϋμό,
γιά τῆς ξε-, τῆς ξενητειᾶς τά μέροι
πού εἶναι τό, πού εἶναι τό δικό μου ταῖρι.

5 Μιά 'μέραν ἐκοιμώμουνα
κι ὄνειρ᾽ ὀνειρευώμουνα,

πώς ἦλθε τό πουλί μου
μέσα εἰς τήν καμαρή μου.

Μέ κάθησε στά γόνατα,
10 μέ δάκρυα στά ὄμματα,
καί ν-ἀρχώνησε νά κλαίη,
τά παράπονα τά λέει.

—Πουλάκι μο' λυπήτερο,
ποῦ ἤσουνα τόσον καιρό;
15 —'Ημουνα μακρυά στά ξένα
καί ἐδούλευα γιά σένα,

γιά νά σοῦ φέρω τά φλουριά,
κόρη μέ τά ξανθά μαλλιά,
νά σοῦ φέρω τό φουστάνι,
20 σάν κι σένα δέν εἰν' ἄλλη.

ONCE MORE LET ME BEGIN TO TELL
(Emigration song)

Once more let me begin to tell
about the sorrow of love,
about the foreign lands
where my own mate is.

5 One day I was sleeping
and I dreamed a dream—
how my little bird
came into my bedroom.

He sat me on his knees,
10 with tears in his eyes,
and he began to cry
and tell me his troubles.

"My sad little bird,
where have you been so long?"
15 "I've been far away in the foreign lands
working for you,

so I could bring you florins,
girl with blonde hair,
so I could bring you a skirt—
20   there's no one like you."

65. ΚΑΤΩ ΣΤΟΝ ΑΣΠΡΟ ΠΟΤΑΜΟ

Κερετσούλα Καραγγιόξη
Σκόπελος

Κάτω στόν ἄσπρο ποταμό
ἄγγελοι παίζουν στό νερό,
πού εἶναι, π'εἶναι πέρδικες κοπαδιά
ν-εἰς τά πρά-, ν-εἰς τά πράσινα πλατάνια.

5   Ξανθομαλλοῦσα κοπηλλιά
μέ χαμηλή μαντηλῶσα,
τή προῖκα της λευκαίνει,
ν-ἡ ζαχαροζυμωμένη.

Μέ τή γλυκειά της τή φωνή
10 ν-ἀρχύησε νά τραγωδῆ,
καί τά πουλιά σωπαίνουν
ν'ἀκούγο' νά μαθαίνουν.

Ν-ἀντίκρυ ἐμορφος βοσκός
παρατηρεῖ ἐκστατικός
15 τή κοπηλλιά πού πλένει,
τή ζαχαρωζυμωμένη.

—Ν-ἄσι, τῆς λέει, κοπηλλιά,
τό πλύσιμο καί τά προικειά,
καί ἔλα μ' ἐμέ νά μένης
20 καί ταῖρι μου νά γύνης.

Ν-ἔχω κοπάδια στό βουνό
καί θᾶσ' ἡ πρώτη στό χωριό
καί πρώτη μέσ' στήν χώρα
ν-ἀπό τά πολλά τά δῶρα.

25 Καί ἡ κοπηλλιά μέ τή φωνή
κι ἀπ' τή ντροπή της σιγανή,
γυρίζει καί τό λέει,
καί ἀπ' τήν ντροπή της κλαίγει.

—Ν-ἔχω πατέρα κι ἀδελφό·
30 σῦρε καί πήγυνε σ᾽ αὐτο᾽ς
    ἄν θέλης νά μέ πάρης,
    ταῖρι σου γιά νά μέ κάνης.

DOWN BY THE WHITE RIVER

Down by the white river,
angels are playing in the water;
there's a flock of partridges
in the green plane trees.

5   A blonde girl
    with lowered headscarf
    is bleaching her dowry,
    the sugary-sweet thing.

    With her sweet voice
10 she began to sing,
    and all the birds hushed
    to listen and to learn.

    Over there a handsome shepherd
    watches ecstatically
15 the girl who is washing,
    the sugary-sweet thing.

    He says to her, "Leave
    the washing and the dowry
    and come live with me
20 and be my mate.

    I've got flocks on the mountain,
    and you'll be the first lady of the village
    and first lady of the countryside
    from all the [wedding] gifts."

25 And the girl with the voice,
    with gentle shyness

turns and speaks to him
and, in her embarrassment, weeps.

"I've got a father and a brother—
30 go to them
if you want to marry me
and make me your mate."

66. ΚΑΛΑΝΤΑ ΤΩΝ ΧΡΙΣΤΟΥΓΕΝΝΩΝ

Κερετσούλα Καραγγιόξη μέ χορωδία
Σκόπελος

Χρι- στού-γεν - να,___ πρω - τού - γεν -να,_____ πρώτ'

ἐ - ορ - τή   τοῦ   χρό - - νου. [2] Γιά

Χριστούγεννα, πρωτόγεννα, πρώτ' ἑορτή τοῦ χρόνου.
Γιά βγῆτε, δέτε, μάθετε ν-ὅπου Χριστός γεννᾶται,
γεννᾶται κι ἀνατρέφεται μέ μέλι καί μέ γάλα·
τό μέλι τρώνε ἄρχοντες, τό γάλα οἱ ἀφεντάδες.
5 Κι ἀνοῖχτε τά κουτάκια σας, τά κατακλειδωμένα,
καί δῶστε μας τόν κόπο μας ἀπ' τό χρυσό πουγγί σας.
'Ἀν εἶσθ' ἀπό τούς πλούσιους, φλωριά μήν τά λυπᾶσθε·
κι ἄν εἶσθ' ἀπό τούς δεύτερους, τάλληρα καί δραχμίτσες·
κι ἄν εἶσθ' ἀπό τούς πάμπτωχούς, ἕνα ζευγάρι κότες.
10 Καί σᾶς καλονυχτίζουμε, πέσε καί κοιμηθῆτε.
. . . .
Στήν ἐκκλησία τρέξατε μ' ὅλον τήν προθυμίαν
καί τοῦ Θεοῦ ν' ἀκούσετε τήν θείαν λειτουργίαν.

KALANDA FOR CHRISTMAS

Christ's birth, first birth, first holiday of the year.
Come out and see and learn that Christ is born,
born and bred with milk and honey—
the nobles eat the honey, the nobles' wives the milk.

5 Now open up your little double-locked boxes
and give us our reward from your golden pocket.
If you're one of the rich, don't be stingy with florins,
if you're of the second class, *talira* and little *drachmas*,
and if you're one of the poorest, a couple of hens.
10 And we bid you goodnight, fall down and go to sleep,

. . . .

Then run to church with all willingness
and listen to the holy liturgy of God.

H ΚΡΗΤΗ

CRETE

67. ΠΟΤΕ ΘΑ ΚΑΝΕ ΞΑΣΤΕΡΙΑ

Ἀδαμαντία Συντυχάκη
Λασηθίου (μαγνητοφώνησε στήν
Βάρη, Σύρου)

Πότε θά κά-, μωρέ, πότε θά κάνη ξαστεριά;
'Έ, πότε θά φλεβαρίση,[1] πότε θά φλεβαρίση;
Νά πάρω τό, νά πάρω τό ντουφέκι μου,

[1] Θά Φλεβαρίση = θά ἔλθη Φεβουάριο.

Νὰ πάρω τό, μωρέ, νὰ πάρω τό ντουφέκι μου,
 ἔ, τὴν ἔμορφη πατρώνα,[2]τὴν ἔμορφη πατρώνα,
νὰ κατέβω, νὰ κατέβω στόν Ὁμαλό,

νὰ κατέβω στόν Ὁμαλό, στὴ στράτα τῶν Μουσούρω',
νὰ κάνω μάνες δίχως γιούς, γυναῖκες δίχως ἄντρες,
5 νὰ κάνω καί μωρά παιδιά νᾶναι δίχως μανάδες,
νὰ κλαῖν' τὴ νύχτα γιά νερό καί τό πρωί γιά γάλα,
καί τ' ἀποξημερώματα γιά τὴ γλυκειά τους μάνα,
μάνα γλυκειά.

WHEN WILL THE SKIES CLEAR?

When will the skies clear, when will February come?
So I can take up my rifle, my beautiful *patrona*,
and go down to the plain of Omalo, to the road of the Mousouron clan,
so I can make mothers sonless, wives husbandless,
5 so I can make little children motherless,
crying in the night for water, in the morning for milk,
and in the early dawn for their sweet mother.

---

[2] Πατρώνα = φυσιγγιοθήκη ἡ ὄνομα τοῦ ὁπλοῦ. (Βλ. Γ. Κ. Σπυριδάκη, Γ. Α. Μέγα καί Δ. Πετροπούλου, Ἑλληνικά Δημοτικά Τραγούδια, I, 273.)

68. ΤΡΑΓΟΥΔΙ ΤΟΥ ΓΑΜΟΥ

'Αδαμαντία Συντυχάκη
Λασηθίου (μαγνητοφώνησε στήν
Βάρη, Σύρου)

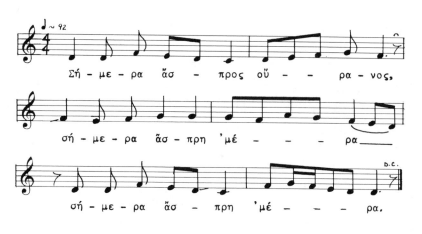

Σήμερα ἄσπρος οὐρανος, σήμερα ἄσπρη 'μέρα, *σήμερα ἄσπρη 'μέρα,*
σήμερα στεφανώνεται ἀητός τήν περιστέρα, <u>ἀητός τήν περιστέρα.</u>

Χρυσά πουλάκια κελαϊδοῦν εἰς τά παράθυρά σας
καί λέμε καλορρίζικα νᾶναι τά στέφανά σας.

5   Νύφη μου, τά στεφάνια σου εἶναι λεμονανθένια,
καί στά παιδιά σου εὔχομαι νᾶναι μαλαματένια.

Γαμπρέ, μιά χάρη σοῦ ξητῶ καί θέλω νά τό κάνης,
τό ρόδο πού σοῦ δώσαμε, νά μή μᾶς τό μαράνης.

Σὰν τὴν Ἁγία Τράπεζα ποὺ εἶναι στερεωμένη,
10 ἔτσι νὰ στερεώσετε καὶ νᾶστ᾽ εὐτυχυσμένοι.

WEDDING SONG

Today white sky, today white day,
today the eagle marries the dove.

Little golden birds are singing at your windows
and we say, "May your wedding wreaths be lucky."

5 My bride, your wedding wreaths are made of lemon blossoms—
may your children's be made of gold.

Groom, I ask one favor of you and I want you to do it:
the rose we have given you, don't let her wither.

As the Holy Communion Table is strong,
10 so may the bonds of marriage be strong and may you be happy.

69. ΜΑΝΤΙΝΑΔΕΣ

Γιάννης Δερμιτζάκης, λύρα
Σητεία

"Αν δῆς στόν ὕ-, ____ ἄν δῆς στόν ὕπ-νο ____ σου δέν-
σέ-, ____ Θἅ-ναι γιά σέ-να ____ βά-σα-

λύρα
τρα
να

"Αν δῆς στόν ὕπ - νο σου ____ δέν - τρα ____
Θἄ - ναι γιά σέ - να βα - σα - να ____

λύρα
γύ - ρω δά μα - ρα - μέ - - να,
πολ-λοί καυ-μοί γιά μέ - - να.

θἅ - ναι γιά

' Ἀν δῆς στόν ὔ-, ἄν δῆς στόν ὕπνο σου δέντρα,
ἄν δῆς στόν ὕπνο σου δέντρα γύρω δά μαραμένα,
θᾶναι γιά σέ-, θᾶναι γιά σένα βάσανα,
θᾶναι γιά σένα βάσανα, πολλοί καϋμοί γιά μένα.

' Ἀν δῆς στόν ὔ-, ἄν δῆς στόν ὕπνο σου θεριά,
θεριά αὐτοί πώς ἔρχονται κοντά σου,
ἐχθροί θά σοῦ, ἐχθροί θά σοῦ πληγόσουνε,
ἐχθροί θά σοῦ πληγόσουνε . . . .

MANDINADHES

If you see trees in your sleep, withered all around,
there'll be troubles for you and sorrows for me.

If you see wild beasts in your sleep, coming close to you,
enemies will wound you . . . .

70. ΜΑΝΤΙΝΑΔΕΣ

Γιάννης Δερμιτζάκης, βιολί
Σητεία

"Ε - λα, δέν ἔ - χεις, φαί - νε - ται, καρ - διά μέ -
βιολί
- σα στό ντέ - φι δι - ό - λου,

"Ε - λα μέ -
σα στό ντέ - φι δι - ό - λου, μέ - - σα

στό ντέ - φι δι - ό - λου, Για - τί θω - ρεῖς πώς

καί - γο - μαι καί δέν μι - λεῖς κα - θό - λου.

Ἔλα, δέν ἔχεις, φαίνεται, καρδιά μέσα στό ντέφι[1] διόλου,
ἔλα, μέσα στό ντέφι διόλου, μέσα στό ντέφι διόλου,
γιατί θωρεῖς πώς καίγομαι καί δέν μιλεῖς καθόλου.

Σάν πέρδικα ἐπλούμισες κι ὁ κόσμος ἐθαυμάζει,
κι ὅποιο γεράκι κι ἄν σέ δῆ ἀπάνω σου κοιτάζει.

5   Σάν τό γεράκι κάθομαι καί σέ παραμονεύω,
κι τό Θεό, στά νύχια μου νά πέσης, ἱκετεύω.

Σάν τό γεράκι θά χυθῶ στά νύχια νά σ' ἁρπάξω
ἀπό τή γᾶ πού κάθησαι κι ὕστερα νά πετάξω.

Ὄντε θά σ' ἔχω δίπλα μου, φεύγουν οἱ ὧρες πᾶνε
10   κι ὄντε θά φύγεις οἱ στιγμές, χρόνια 'ναι, δέν περνᾶνε.

MANDINADHES

It seems you've got no heart at all—
you see me burning up and you don't say a word.

You've decked yourself out like a partridge, and everyone admires
    you,
and if a hawk catches sight of you, he'll stop and stare.

5   Like the hawk I sit here, lying in wait for you,
and I entreat God to make you fall into my clutches.

Like a hawk I'm going to swoop down and seize you
from the earth where you're sitting, and then I'll fly away.

When you're beside me the hours speed by,
10   but when you leave seconds seem like years and don't pass.

---

[1] Μεταφορά διά στῆθος;

71. ΜΑΝΤΙΝΑΔΕΣ

Γιάννης Δερμιτζάκης, βιολί
Σητεία

Εἶ - σαι   σου - πιά   καί   τρι - γυρ - νᾶς   στῆς
Μά   θά   βρε - θῆς   καμ - μιά   στιγ - μή   χω -

βάρ - κας   μου   τήν   κό - χη,
ρίς   νά   θές   στ᾽ ά - πό - χη.

Εἶσαι σουπιά καί τριγυρνᾶς στῆς βάρκας μου τήν κόχη,
μά θά βρεθῆς καμμιά στιγμή χωρίς νά θές στ᾽ ἀπόχη.

Εἶμαι ψαρᾶς κι εἶσαι σουπιά, νά σ᾽ ἔχα στό τηγάνι,
μ᾽ ὅλο μέ βλέπις καί γλακᾶς καί μοῦ πετᾶς μελάνι.

MANDINADHES

You're a cuttlefish circling round the hull of my boat,
but sometime, without wanting to, you're going to fall into my net.

I'm a fisherman, you're a cuttlefish—I wish I had you in my frying
  pan;
but you see me and run away and squirt ink at me.

Η ΔΩΔΕΚΑΝΗΣΟΣ

DODECANESE ISLANDS

72. ΚΑΤΩ ΧΟΡΟΣ (Τοῦ γάμου)

Ντίνα Σάββενα
Ρόδος

"Ε__ βρ'ά-μάν ά - μάν ά - μάν, αὐ - τός ὁ__

γά - μος ἕ - πρε - πε__ "Ε ____ αὐ -

τός ὁ γά - - - μος ἕ - πρε-πε να

γί - νη__ στήν 'Ελ-λά - δα, "Ω,__ νά

γί - νη__ στήν __ 'Ελ - λά - δα__

"Ε____ βρ'ά-μάν ά - μάν ά - μάν, γιά νά - - κλου-

θή - ση ὁ βα - ση - - λιᾶς, "Ε - λα, γιά

'Έ, βρ' ἀμάν, ἀμάν, ἀμάν, αὐτός ὁ γάμος ἔπρεπε,
ἔ, αὐτός ὁ γάμος ἔπρεπε νά γίνη στήν Ἑλλάδα, ὤ, νά γίνη στήν
  Ἑλλάδα,
ἔ, βρ' ἀμάν, ἀμάν, ἀμάν, γιά ν' ἀκλουθήση ὁ βασιληᾶς,
ἔλα, γιά ν' ἀκλουθήσ' ὁ βασιληᾶς κι ὅλοι ἡ Δωδεκάδα, ὤ, κι ὅλοι ἡ
  Δωδεκάδα.

Νυφούλα, τό βελάκι σου, ἄγγελοι σοῦ τ' ὄραψα'
καί στήν δεξιά σου τή μεριά τόν ἄγγελον[1] ἔγραψα'.

KATO DANCE (Wedding song)

This wedding should have taken place in Greece
so the king could have attended and all his twelve ministers.

Little bride, angels sewed your jacket for you,
and at the right side they inscribed [your husband's name].

[1] Τόν ἄντρα σου; (βλ. Α. Πουλιανοῦ, Λαϊκά Τραγούδια τῆς Ἰκαρίας, 199).

73. ΤΕΣΣΑΡΑ ΦΥΛΛΑ ΕΧΕΙ Η ΚΑΡΔΙΑ, ΜΑΡΙΤΣΑ ΜΟΥ

Ντίνα Σάββενα
Ρόδος

Τέσ - σα - ρα   φύλ - λα   ἔχ' ἡ   καρ - διά, Μα -

ρί - τσα μου,   Τά _____ δυό, _____ τά

δυό τά - χεις παρ - μέ - - να,   μέ - να,

Τέσσαρα φύλλα ἔχ' ἡ καρδιά, Μαρίτσα μου,
τά δυό, τά δυό τάχεις παρμένα,
καί τἄλλα δυό μου τάφησες, Μαρίτσα μου,
γιά πα-, γιά πάντα μαραμένα.

Μή μοῦ ξυπνᾶς τό παρελθό, ἄσε το νά κοιμᾶται,
γιατί πολύ ἡ καρδιά τά πάντα νά θυμᾶται.

THE HEART'S GOT FOUR LEAVES, MARITSA

The heart's got four leaves, Maritsa; you've taken two of them
and left me the other two forever withered.

Don't wake up the past, leave it sleeping,
because my heart remembers everything.

74. ΣΑΝ ΠΑΗΣ, ΚΟΡΗ, ΣΤΟ ΝΕΡΟ

Ντίνα Σάββενα
Ρόδος

Σάν πά - ης κό - ρη,＿＿ σάν πά - ης κό - ρη,

Σάν πά - ης κό - ρη ＿＿＿ κό - ρη στό＿＿ νε -

ρό＿ Σάν πά - ης κό - ρη στό＿＿ νε-

ρό＿ Νά τό γε - μί - σης δρο - σε - ρό.

Σάν πάης, κόρη, σάν πάης, κόρη,
σάν πάης, κόρη, κόρη, στό νερό,
σάν πάης, κόρη, στό νερό
νά τό γεμίσης δροσερό.

' Άν δέν τό φέρω, άν δέν τό φέρω,
άν δέν τό φέρω, μάνα, δροσερό,
άν δέν τό φέρω δροσερό
τά νειάτα μου νά μή χαρῶ.

WHEN YOU GO TO THE WATERING PLACE

"When you go to the watering place, daughter,
be sure to get cool water."

"If I don't bring back cool water, mother,
may I not enjoy my youth."

75. ΚΑΝΤΑΔΑ

Χρύσα Σαρίδ ου
Ρόδ ος

"Ω Ρό - δο μου _____ πε - - ρή-

φα - - - νη _____ μέ τά ψη -

λά _____ βου - - νά _____ σου _____ 'Η ξε - νη - τει-

ά τά χαί - ρε - - ται_ τά λε - βεν

το - - - παι - δά _____ σου.

'' Ὦ Ρόδ ο μου περήφανη μέ τά ψηλά βουνά σου,
ἡ ξενητειά τά χαίρεται τά λεβεντοπαιδά σου.

Κρήτη μέ τά καράβια σου, Σάμο μέ τίς ἐληές σου,
Ρόδ ο μέ τά ψηλά βουνά καί μέ τίς κοπελλιές σου.

5 Μέ ξέχασε ἡ ἀγάπη μου, μανούλα μου, στά ξένα·
   μέ γέλασε, μέ ξέχασε κι ἀλοίμονο σέ μένα.

   Θά πάρω κάμπους καί βουνά χωρίς νά ξαποστάσω
   νά βρῶ ποτάμι λησμονιᾶς νά πιῶ νά σέ ξεχάσου.

KANDADHA

Proud Rhodes with your tall mountains,
the foreign lands salute your brave children.

Crete with your boats, Samos with your olive trees,
Rhodes with your tall mountains and beautiful girls.

5 My love forgot me in the foreign lands, *manoula*,
   poor me, she laughed at me and forgot me.

I'll take to the fields and mountains
to find the river of forgetfulness, to drink and forget you.

76. ΤΟ ΠΕΡΙΒΟΛΙ (Τοῦ γάμου)

Μαρία Λακλαριδου
Νίσυρος (μαγνηταφώνησε στήν
Ρόδο)

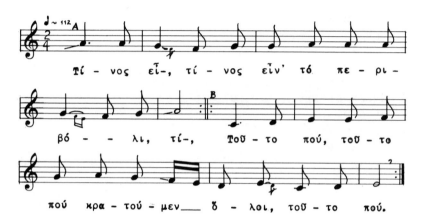

Τί - νος εἶ-, τί - νος εἶν' τό πε - ρι -

βό - - λι, τί-, Τοῦ - το πού, τοῦ - το

πού κρα - τού - μεν____ ὄ - λοι, τοῦ - το πού.

Τ ίνος εἶ-, τίνος εἶν' τό περιβόλι, τί-,
τοῦτο πού, τοῦτο πού κρατούμεν ὄλοι, τοῦτο πού.

Τ' ἄρχοντα Χαζημανώλη[1]
κι ἔδωσε τα τοῦ γαμπροῦ του
5 τ' ἄξιου τ' ἀξιαζουμένου του.
Στήν πέρα δίπλα τοῦ χοροῦ
μαντῆλιν ηὖρα, τίνος εἶν';
Καί τοῦ νιογαμπροῦ μας εἶναι

[1] ' Ὀνομα τοῦ πατέρα τῆς νύφης.

κι ἔπεσεν ἀπ᾽ τά λινά του
10 κι ἀφ᾽ τά λινομέταξά του.

THE ORCHARD (Wedding song)

Whose is this orchard
where we're all gathered?
It belongs to the noble Khazimanoli,
and he gave it to the groom,
5 his worthy son-in-law.
There at the edge of the dance
I found a kerchief, whose is it?
It belongs to our new groom,
and it fell from his linen,
10 from his silk linen.

77. Α·Ι·ΝΤΕ, ΠΑΡΕ, ΦΡΑΝΤΖΗ (Τοῦ γάμου)

Μαρία Λακλαρίδου
Νίσυρος (μαγνητοφώνησε στήν Ρόδο)

"Αϊν - τε, πά - ρε, Φραν - τζῆ τή λύ-, ν'ἀ-μάν ἀ - μάν βο-ή - θα Πα - να - γιά, Πά - ρε Φραν-τζῆ τή λύ - ρα σου, "Αϊν - τε, πά - ρε Φραν - τζῆ τή λύ - ρα σου κ'ἐ - γώ τό, κ'ἐ - γώ τόν τα - μπού - ρα μου, κ'ἐ-, κ'ἐ- μου.

'Άϊτε, πάρε, Φραντζῆ, τή λύ-,
  ν-ἀμάν, ἀμάν, βοήθα Παναγιά,
πάρε, Φραντζῆ, τή λύρα σου,
ἄϊτε, πάρε Φραντζῆ, τή λύρα σου,
  κ' ἐγώ τό, κ' ἐγώ τόν ταμπούρα μου, κ' ἐ-,
  κ' ἐγώ τό, κ' ἐγώ τόν ταμπούρα μου,
ἄϊτε, νά πά' νά ξεφαντώ-,
  ν-ἀμάν, ἀμάν, βοήθα Παναγιά,
νά πά' νά ξεφαντώσωμε,
ἄϊτε, νά πά' νά ξεφαντώσωμε
  κάτω στῆς, κάτω στῆς πεθερᾶς μου.

Πάλι περνῶ το, τό στενό, τό σεβνταλῆ σοκάκι
ποὺ δέν ἐπέρασε κανείς νά μήν ἀναστενάξη.

GET YOUR *LYRA*, FRANDZI

Get your *lyra*, Frandzi, and I'll get my *tamboura*,
and we'll go feast ourselves down at my mother-in-law's.

Again I take the narrow path, the love-sick lane
where no one has ever passed by without sighing.

78. ΤΩΡΑ ΤΑ ΠΟΥΛΙΑ (Τοῦ γάμου)

Γιάννης Συνέσιος
Χ. Ἀντιμάχεια, Κῶ

'Μέ - ρα μέ-, _____ μέ - - ε - ρα

μέ - - - ρω - ω - σε, _____

'μέ - ρα μέ - ρω - σε__ Τώ - ρα ἡ αὐ - γή χα -

ρά - - - - ζει, Τώ - - ρα

τά, _____ τώ - - ρα τά _____

τώ - ρα τά__ που - λιά, [2] Τώ - ρα

'Μέρα μέ-, 'μέρα μέρωσε, 'μέρα μέρωσε,
τώρα ἡ αυγή χαράζει,
τώρα τά, τώρα τά, τώρα τά πουλιά,

τώρα τά, τώρα τά πουλιά, τώρα τά πουλιά,
τώρα τά χελιδόνια,
5 τώρα οἱ πέ-, τώρα οἱ πέ-, τώρα οἱ πέρδικες,

τώρα οἱ πέρδικες,
τώρα οἱ περδικοπούλες,
τώρα κελαϊδούν.

NOW THE BIRDS ARE SINGING
(Wedding song)

Day begins,
now the dawn breaks,
now the birds,
now the swallows,
5 now the partridges,
now the baby partridges,
now they're all singing.

1. Yioryios Tsetsos, Singer from the Village of Metsovon, Epiros

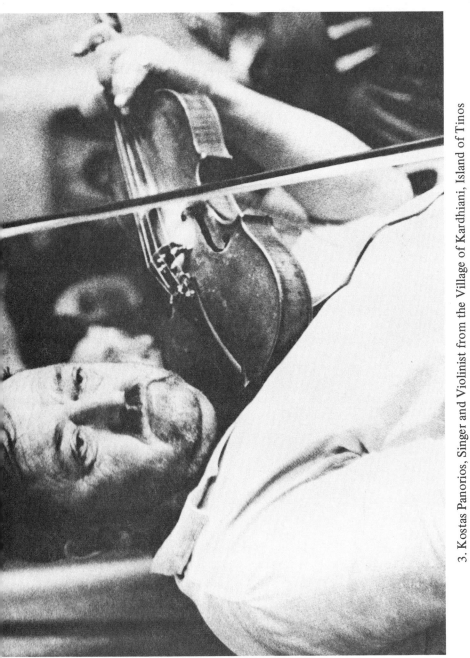

3. Kostas Panorios, Singer and Violinist from the Village of Kardhiani, Island of Tinos

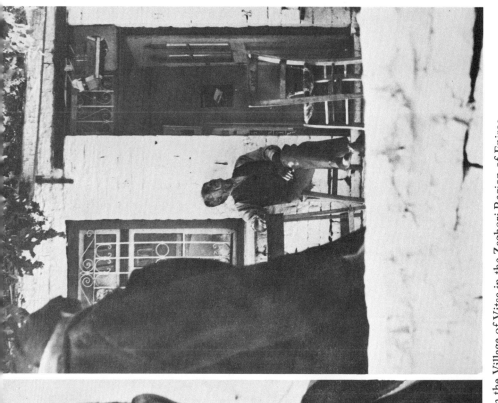
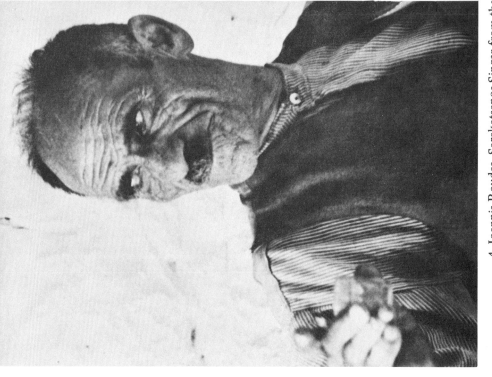

4. Ioannis Roudas, Sarakatsanos Singer from the Village of Vitsa in the Zaghori Region of Epiros

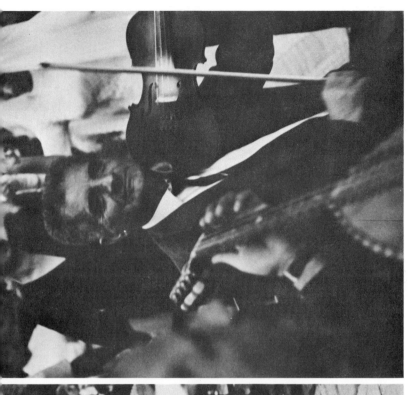

5. Wedding Dance in a Zaghori Village

6. Two Women, Village of Vitsa

7. Sarakatsanos Hut in a Zaghori Villa

79. ΤΡΑΓΟΥΔΙ ΤΗΣ ΝΥΦΗΣ

Γιάννης Συνέσιος
Χ. Ἀντιμάχεια, Κῶ

"Ε-ρι, ν-ῆ-βγεν ἡ νύ - φη_____ ν-ῆ-βγεν ἡ νυ-

φη, Ν-ῆ-βγεν ἡ νύ - φη_ στό χο - ρό, ν-ῆ-,

ἔ-ρι, -βγεν ἡ νύ-φη στό χο-ρό, ν-ῆ-βγεν νά συρ-για-

νί - ση, ν-ῆ - βγεν νά συρ - για-νί - ση, ν-ῆ-

"Ερι, ν-ῆβγεν ἡ νύφη, ν-ῆβγεν ἡ νύφη,
ν-ῆβγεν ἡ νύφη στό χορό, ν-ῆ-,
ἔρι, -βγεν ἡ νύφη στό χορό,
ν-ῆβγεν νά συργιανίση, ν-ῆ-
-βγεν νά συργιανίση, ν-ῆ-,
ἔ, ν-ῆβγεν νά δῆ, ν-ῆβγεν νά δῆ τές,
ν-ῆβγεν νά δῆ τές 'λευτερές, ν-ῆ-,

ἔρι, -βγεν νὰ δῆ τές 'λευτερές,
νὰ ν-τές 'ποχαιρετήση, ν-ἠ̣-,
-βγεν νὰ ουργιανίση, ν-ἠ̣-.

''Ερι, ν-ὡς λάμπουν τζ' ἀχτι-, γειά 'Λένη μου, γειά 'Λένη,
ν-ὡς λάμπουν τζ' ἀχτινοβολοῦν, ν-ὡ-,
ἔρι, -ς λάμπουν τζ' ἀχτινοβολοῦν
   στὸν οὐρανόν τ' ἄστρα, στὸν
   οὐρανον τ' ἄστρα, στόν,
ἔρι, μ-ἔτσι λάμπει, γειά 'Λένη μου, γειά 'Λένη,
μ-ἔτσι λάμπει τζ' ἡ νύφη μας, μ-ἔ-,
ἔρι, μ-ἔτσι λάμπει τζ' ἡ νύφη μας
   ντυμένη μέσα στ' ἄσπρα, ντυμένη μέσα στ' ἄσπρα, ντυ-.

BRIDE'S SONG

The bride came out to the dance to promenade,
she came out to see the free girls, to say good-bye to them.

As the stars in the sky shine and radiate,
so our bride shines, all dressed in white.

80. ΤΡΑΓΟΥΔΙ ΤΟΥ ΓΑΜΟΥ

Γιάννης Συνέσιος
Χ. Ἀντιμάχεια, Κῶ

"Ε-ρι, ἔ - λα ἡ ὤ - ρα, ἄχ, ἡ κα - λή___ στό

πό - διο___ τσ'ἡ νύ-μ'α μας   Τσ'ἡ Πα-να -

γί - α___ τσι ὁ Χρι - στός___ δε - ξιά___ τσ'ἀρ - -

ρι - στε - ρά μας.   "Ε-ρι,   Πα - να - γιά τσι_'Α -

α - πό - στο-λοι, Νἄρ-θε-τε στό νυ-φό - στο-λι.

' Ἔρι, ἔλα ἡ ὥρα, ἄχ, ἡ καλή, στό πόδιο τσ' ἡ νυμ[φ]α μας
Τσ' ἡ Παναγιά τσι ὁ Χριστός δεξιά τσι ἀρριστερά μας.

᾿῎Ερι, Παναγιά τσι ᾿Απόστολοι,
νᾶρθετε στό νυφόστολι.

5 ᾿῎Ερι, καράβ᾿ εἶναι τόνο σπίτι σας, λιμάν᾿ εἰν᾿ ἡ αὐλή σας,
κ᾿ ἐμεῖς ἐδῶ πού ἤρθαμε γιά χάρω τήν δική σας.
  ᾿῎Ερι, προβάλετε, προβάλετε
γιά νά μᾶς περιλάβετε.

WEDDING SONG

Come blessed hour, standing there is our bride,
and to our right and left the Virgin and Christ.
  Virgin and Apostles,
  come to the bride's dressing room.

5 Your house is a boat, your courtyard a harbor,
and we have come here for your sake.
  Come out
  and receive us.

81. ΤΡΑΓΟΥΔΙ ΠΟΥ ΞΥΡΙΣΕΤΑΙ Ο ΓΑΜΠΡΟΣ

Γιάννης Σινέσιος
Χ. Ἀντιμάχεια, Κῶ

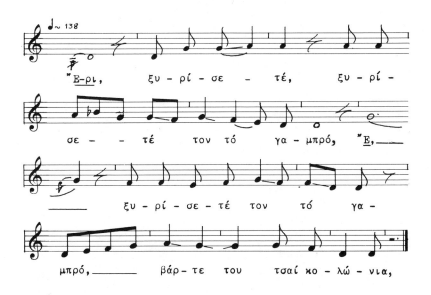

'' Ερι, ξυρίσετέ, ξυρίσετέ τον τό γαμπρό,
έ, ξυρίσετέ τον τό γαμπρό, βάρτε του τσέ κολώνια,
έρι, νά τοῦ 'φχηθού-, νά τοῦ 'φχητούμεν ὅλοι,
έ, νά τοῦ 'φχηθούμεν ὅλοι μας νά ζήση χίλια χρόνια.

'' Ερι, μπαρμπέρι, τό, μπαρμπέρη, τό ξυράφι σου,
έ, μπαρμπέρη, τό ξυράφι σου, νά τοῦ μαλαματώσης,

γιά νά ξυρί-, γιά νά ξυρίσης τό γαμπρό,
ἔρι, νά τό μαλαματώσης, νά μήν τόν ἐλαβώσης.

SONG FOR SHAVING THE GROOM

Shave the groom, put cologne on him
so we can all wish him a thousand-year life.

Barber, gild your razor
so you can shave the groom and not wound him.

82. ΣΑΝ ΠΑΣ ΣΤΑ ΞΕΝΑ, ΑΓΑΠΕ ΜΟΥ (Τῆς ξενητειᾶς)

Γιώργιος Πέτρος
Χ. Ἀντιμάχεια, Κῶ

τοῦ___ χω - ρισ-μοῦ_____ τόν πό - - - νο.

Σάν πᾶς στά ξένα, πάρε κ᾽ ἐμένα,
πάρε κ᾽ ἐμένα γιά συντροφιά.
Σάν πᾶς στά ξένα, ἀγάπε μου, μή κάψης ἕνα χρόνο,
γιατί δέν θά ταγεντιθῶ[1] τοῦ χωρισμοῦ τόν πόνο.

5   Σάν πᾶς στά ξένα, πάρε κ᾽ ἐμένα
στήν ἀγκαλιά σου γιά συντροφιά σου.
Δακρύζουνε τά μάτια μου καί κλαίει κ᾽ ἡ καρδιά μου
σάν κάτσω καί συλλογιστῶ πῶς φεύγεις μακρυά μου.

Καί μέ τά τόσα καί μ᾽ ἄλλα τόσα
10 βάσανα, ἄχ, πού μέ πλακώσαν.

WHEN YOU GO OFF TO THE FOREIGN LANDS
(Emigration song)

When you go off to the foreign lands, take me, too,
take me along for company.
When you go off to the foreign lands, don't stay for more than a year
because I can't stand the pain of separation.

5   When you go off to the foreign lands, take me, too,
in your arms, for company.

[1] Θά ταγεντιθῶ = θά ὑποφέρω (λ.τ. dayanmak).

My eyes fill with tears, and my heart is crying
as I sit here and think about how you're going far away from me.

And with the many and again as many
10   troubles that crush me.

83. Η ΕΛΕΝΗ

Νικόλαος Αἰγουλᾶς
Χ. Ἀντιμάχεια, Κῶ

"Ερ-χο-μαι ἔ - μπρός τήν πόρ-τα σου, 'Ε -
λέ - νη μ', 'Ο - σάν τό ζη - τια - - νά -
κι εἶμ', ἔρ - χο - μαι, "Αχ,___
σύ μπα - - ξές,___ συ μπα-ξές___
κ'ἐ - γώ φυ - τά - νι· Νά σέ___
ἀ - γα-, νά σέ ἀ-, ὤ, -ἀ - - - -
γα - α - πῶ δέν κά - νει. [2] "Ε___

'' Ερχομαι ἐμπρός τήν πόρτα σου, Ἐλένη μ', ὀσάν τό ζητιανάκι εἰμ',
ἔρχομαι,
'' Ἀχ, σύ μπαξές,[1] σύ μπαξές κ' ἐγώ φυτάνι·
νά σέ ἀγα-, νά σέ ἀγαπῶ δέν κάνει.
ἔ, καί μ' ἔδιωξαν ἡ μάνα σου, Ἐλένη, γιατ' ἤμουνα ξενάκι.
5   '' Ἀχ, πᾶν τά νειᾶτα, πᾶν τά νειᾶτα καί πᾶν τά κάλλη,
δέν ξανα-, δέν ξαναγυρίζουν πάλι.

ELENI

I come before your door, Eleni, like the little beggar that I am,
(You're the garden and I'm the plant—
I'm not supposed to love you.)
and your mother threw me out because I was a stranger.
5   (Youth and beauty go away
and never return.)

[1] Μπαξές = περιβόλι (λ.τ. *bahçe*).

84. ΔΕΝ ΒΡΙΣΚΕΤΑΙ ΠΟΝΟΜΕΤΡΟ

Παναγιώτης Καντόνιος
Χ. Ἀντιμάχεια, Κῶ

' Ἄχ, δέν βρίσκεται πονόμετρο γιά νά μετροῦν τόν πόνο·
ὅσοι τόν ἔχουν στήν καρδιά, 'κεῖνοι τόν ξεύρουν μόνο.

' Ἀχ, τά βάσανα καί οἱ καϋμοί γιά 'μένα γεννήθηκαν·
κι ἄν ἔχω τό πρωΐν χαράν, τό βράδυν ἔχω πίκραν.

THERE'S NO PAIN METER

There's no pain meter to measure pain—
those who have it in their hearts, they alone know it.

Troubles and misfortunes were born just for me,
and, if I have pleasure in the morning, by evening I've got grief.

85. TO EPI

Γιάννης Σινέσιος
Χ. ᾿Αντιμάχεια, Κῶ

"Ε-ρι _____ δέν ἠ - μπο - ρῶ νά, _____

δέν _____ ἠ - μπο - ρῶ νά, Δέν ἠ - μπο - ρῶ

νά _____ κλαί - γω _____ πιά, "Ε-ρι,

δέν ἠ - μπο - ρῶ νά _____ κλαί - γω _____

- ω πιά _____ Μα - ράν - θη-, μα - ράν - θη - κ᾿ ἡ

καρ - διά _____ μου, _____ μα - - - - ράν-θη-

"Ε-ρι _____ κι ἀν-τί _____ καλ - λιά _____

καί_____ ἀν - τί καλ - λιά, καί ἀν -

τί καλ - λιά - - ιά σέ - να - νε,

"Ε-ρι, κι ἀν-τί καλ-λιά___ σέ - να - - νε

χά - νω τά, χά - νω___ τά δα - κρυ - ά

μου,_____ χά - - - νω τά.

''Ερι, δέν ἠμπορῶ νά, δέν ἠμπορῶ νά,
δέν ἠμπορῶ νά κλαίγω πιά,
ἔρι, δέν ἠμπορῶ νά κλαίγω πιά,
   μαράνθη-, μαράνθηκ' ἡ καρδιά μου, μαράνθη-,
ἔρι, κι ἀντί καλλιά, τσέ ἀντί καλλιά,
τσέ ἀντί καλλιά σένανε,
ἔρι, καί ἀντί καλλιά σένανε
   χάνω τά, χάνω τά δακρυά μου, χάνω τά.

''Ερι, δακρυά τρέχουν, δακρυά τρέχουνε,
δακρυά τρέχουν σάν φωτιές,
ὤχ, δακρυά τρέχουν σάν φωτιές

γύρ᾽ ἀπ᾽ τά, γύρ᾽ ἀπ᾽ τά μάγουλά μου, γύρ᾽ ἀπ᾽ τά,
ἔ, τσέ μπέφτουνε στό, καί μπέφτουν στό,
τσέ μπέφτουνε στό στῆθος μου,
ἔρι, τσέ πέφτουνε στό στῆθος μου
    τσέ κάβου᾽, τσέ κάβουν τήν καρδιά μου, τσέ κάβου᾽.

ERI

I can't cry anymore, my heart's withered away
and, in return for your beauty, I lose my tears.

Tears run like fires down my cheeks
and fall onto my breast and burn my heart.

86. ΣΑΝ ΤΟ ΣΒΥΣΜΕΝΟ ΚΑΡΒΟΥΝΟ
(Σιγανό κώτικο)

Γιώργιος Πέτρος
Χ. Ἀντιμάχεια, Κῶ

Ἀχ, σάν τό σβυσμένο, σάν τό σβυσμένο κάρβουνο,
σάν τό σβυσμένο, ἄχ, σάν τό σβυσμένο κάρβουνο

μαυρίσεν, μαυρίσεν ἡ καρδιά μου, μαυρίσεν,
ἄχι, ἀπ' τὰ πολλά μου, ἀπ' τὰ πολλά μου βάσανα,
ἀπ' τὰ πολλά μου, ἄχι, ἀπ' τὰ πολλά μου βάσανα
κι ἀπό τά, κι ἀπό τὰ δακρυά μου,
(κι ἀπό τά, κι ἀπό τὰ δακρυά μου,) κι ἀ-.

Τὰ βάσανα στόν κόσμ' αὐτόν, τὰ παῖζω κουμπολόγι
καί κάνω διασκέδασι τόν πόνο πού μέ τρώει.

LIKE THE BURNT-OUT COAL

Like the burnt-out coal, my heart's turned black
from all my troubles and from my tears.

The troubles of this world are my *koumboloyi* beads,
and I amuse myself with the pain that eats me.

87. ΔΥΟΣΜΑΡΑΚΙ

Γιώργιος Πέτρος
Χ. Ἀντιμάχεια, Κῶ

"Ο - λα τά μά - τια, _____ τά μά - τια
μά - τια - 'ναι, δυοσ-μα - - ρά - κι
μου, "Ωχ, μ' ὅ - λα___ τά χεί - - λη,
χεί - - λη, Σι - γα - νά, σι - γα - νά,
σι - γα - νά καί τα - πει - νά καί τα - πει - νά,

'Ὅλα τά μάτια, τά μάτια μάτια 'ναι, δυοσμαράκι μου,
ὤχ, μ' ὅλα τά χείλη, χείλη,
σιγανά, σιγανά, σιγανά καί ταπεινά καί ταπεινά,

μά ὄλοι οἱ, ἄ-, ἄχ, οἱ ἄνθρωπ' ἔχουνε, δυόσμε τρικλωνέ,
καί ἐμένα δέ μ' ἔχουν,
σιγάνά, σιγανά, οὔτ' ἐχθροί μ' οὔτε καί φίλοι οὔτε καί φίλοι.[1]

Θά ὑποφέρω, -ποφέρω στήν ζωή, δυοσμαράκι μου,
ἀφοῦ ἔτσι τό θέλει,
σιγανά, σιγανά, σιγανά καί ταπεινά καί ταπεινά.
Ἡ ἄπονη σου, καλέ, ἡ καρδιά, δυόσμε τρικλωνέ,
σκληρά νά ὑποφέρω,
σιγανά, σιγανά, σιγανά πατῶ στή γῆ, πατῶ στή γῆ.

LITTLE MINT

All eyes are eyes, all lips, lips,
all men are either enemies or friends.

I endure life because that's the way it is;
your unfeeling heart is hard to bear.

---

[1] Ὁ στίχος 2 εἶναι ἀνακατωμένος· νομίζω σωστά εἶναι:

M'ὄλοι οἱ ἄν-, οἱ ἄνθρωπ' ἔχουνε, δυοσμέ τρικλωνέ,
οὔτ' ἐχθροί οὔτε φίλοι,
σιγανά, σιγανά, σιγανά πατῶ στή γῆ, πατῶ στή γῆ.

88. Ο ΒΟΣΚΟΣ ΚΙ Ο ΒΑΣΙΛΙΑΣ

Μιχαήλ Μπαϊράμπης, τραγοῦδι,
καί Μανώλη Μπαϊράμπης, τσαμπούνα
Κάλυμνος

'Ο βο - σκός, βο - σκός κι ὁ βα - σι - λιᾶς

'Ο βο - σκός_____ βα - σι - - λιᾶς

στοί-χη - μαν ἐ - βά - - ζα - - σι,

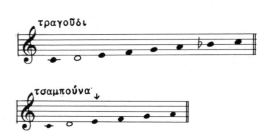

τραγοῦδι

τσαμπούνα

Ὁ βοσκός, ἀμάνι ἀραμάνι,
ὁ βοσκός, βοσκός κι ὁ βασιλιᾶς,
ὁ βοσκός κι ὁ βασιλιᾶς
στοίχημαν ἐβάξασι,

στοίχημαν, ἀμάνι ἀραμάνι,
στοίχημαν, -ημαν ἠβάξασι,
στοίχημαν ʼβάξασι
καί στοιχηματίξασι.

5 —Πές μ᾽, ἀφέ-, ἀμαν ὄιμοι ἀμάνι,
<u>πές μ᾽, ἀφέ-, ἀφέντη βασιλιᾶ,</u>
<u>πές μ᾽, ἀφέντη βασιλιᾶ,</u>
τ᾽εἰν᾽ πού βάζεις στοίχημα;

—Βάζω τή βασιλισσα
μέ τό βασιλίκιw της.
Πές κ᾽ ἐσύ, καλέ βοσκέ,
10 τ᾽εἰν᾽ πού βάζεις στοίχημα;
—Βάζω χίλια πρόβατα
μέ ἀργυροκούδουνα·
βάζω καί καλόν ἀρνί,
μεταξετό τό μαλλί.
15 Σόνταν¹ τά κατέβαζε
ὁ βοσκός τά πρόβατα,
ὁ βοσκός τά πρόβατα
ἀπό τά² λακκώματα,
προβάλλει κ᾽ ἡ βασιλισσα
20 ἀπό μακρυνή θυρί.
—Βασιλ᾽, πού νάμουν βόσκισσα,
μάνα, καί τυροκόσμισσα³
νά καί λάλουν τό μαντρί,
νάκαμα χλωρό τυρί.

THE SHEPHERD AND THE KING

The shepherd and the king
were laying a wager,
laying a wager
and making a bet.
5 "Tell me, *afendi* king,
what will you wager?"
"I'll wager my queen
and her royal lands.

¹ Σόνταν = ὄταν.
² Κάτω στά.
³ Τυροκόμισσα = γυναῖκα πού παρασκευάζει τό τυρί.

Now you tell me, good shepherd,
10 what will you wager?"
"I'll wager a thousand sheep
with silver bells
and my best lamb
with the silklike wool."
15 When the shepherd
brought his sheep,
the shepherd brought his sheep
down to the watering place,
the queen appeared
20 at a far-off window:
"I wish I were a shepherdess
and cheesemaker
so I could hear the birds singing in the *mandri*
and make fresh cheese.

ΟΙ ΚΥΚΛΑΔΕΣ

CYCLADES ISLANDS

89. ΤΡΑΓΟΥΔΙ ΤΗΣ ΒΕΝΤΕΜΑΣ[1]

Πέτρος Χρύσος
Σαντορίνη (μαγνηταφώνησε στή
Βάρη, Σύρου)

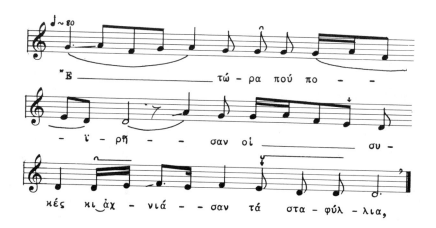

''Ε, τώρα πού ποιηρῆσαν[2] οἱ συκιές κι ἀχνιάσαν[3] τά σταφύλια,
ἔ, θά πάρω τήν ἀγάπη μου νά πάω στήν 'Αθήνα.
Ρέ, τόν κρίνο βάζω στό νερό, τή ζάχαρι στήν κούπα,
ρέ, κι ὥσπου νά λυώση ἡ ζάχαρι, ὡς πάει ἡ ἀγάπη μου.

[1] Βεντέμας = συγκομιδή σταφυλᾶς (λ. ἰταλ. vendemmia).
[2] Ποιηρῆσαν = ἀφθονοῦσε.
[3] 'Αχνιάσαν = χλωνίαξαν.

GRAPE-HARVESTING SONG

Now that the fig trees are full and the grapes have turned pale,
I'll take my love and go to Athens.
I put the lily in the water, the sugar in the cup,
and, by the time the sugar dissolves, my love is gone.

90. ΝΑΝΟΥΡΙΣΜΑ

Εὐαγγελία Κοΐτιζᾶ
Ἑρμούπολις, Σύρου

"Υπ - νε πού παίρ-νεις τά μι - κρά, _____

— ἔ - λα, πά - ρε καί τοῦ - - το_____

''Υπνε πού παίρνεις τά μικρά, ἔλα, πάρε καί τοῦτο.
Μικρό, μικρό σέ τ'ὄδωσα, μεγάλο φέρε μου το·
μεγάλο σάν ψηλό βουνό, ἴσια σάν κυπαρίσσι
κ' οἱ κλῶνοι του ν' ἁπλώνονται σ' ἀνατολή καί δύση.

LULLABY

Sleep, you who take the little ones, come, take this one, too.
Very small I give him to you, bring him back to me big—
big as a tall mountain, straight as a cypress tree,
and may his branches spread from east to west.

91. ΚΑΛΑΝΤΑ ΤΟΥ ΛΑΖΑΡΟΥ

Εὐαγγελία Κοντιζᾶ καί
Μαρίνα Κοντιζᾶ
Ἑρμούπολις, Σύρου

Ἦλθ᾽ ὁ Λάζαρος, ἦλθαν τά βάγια,
ἦλθ᾽ ἡ Κυριακή πού τρῶν τά ψάρια.

—Ποῦσουν, Λάζαρε, ποῦν᾽ ἡ φωνή σου;
πού σέ γύρευε ἡ μάνα κ᾽ ἡ ἀδελφή σου.

5   —᾽Ἤμουνα στή γῆ, στή γῆ χωμένος
κι ἀπό τούς νεκρούς, νεκρούς ἀναστημένου᾽.

Δῶστε μου νερό, νερό λιγάκι
νά ξεπλύνω τῆς καρδιᾶς μου τό φαρμάκι.

Δῶστε μας αὐγά, αὐγά νά σᾶς τά ποῦμε,
10   κ᾽ οἱ κοτίτσες σας πολλά γενοῦνε,
κ᾽ οἱ φωλίτσες σας δέν τά χωροῦνε.

Καί τοῦ χρόνου.

KALANDA FOR LAZARUS DAY

Lazarus Day has come, Palm Sunday has come,
the Sunday we eat fish has come.

"Where were you, Lazarus, where's your voice?
Your mother and your sister were looking for you."

5 "I was buried in the earth
and I am risen from the dead.

Give me a little water
to clean the poison out of my heart."

Give us some eggs now that we sang for you
10 and your hens have laid so many
and your nests don't have room for them all.

92. ΚΑΛΑΝΤΑ ΤΗΣ ΠΡΩΤΟΧΡΟΝΙΑΣ

Πενελόπη Σκιαδᾶ
Χ. Πρόδρομος, Πάρου

Μά 'μεῖς δέν ἦλ - θα - με ἐ - δῶ
νά_____ φᾶ-, νά φᾶ - με καί νά πιού-με,
[2] Μό-νο σᾶς ἀ - - γα-πού - σα - με,
κ' ἦλ - θα-, κ' ἦλ-θα - με νά σᾶς δοῦ - με.
[19] Καί στόν κό-, καί στόν κόσ - μο ξα - κουσμέ - νος.

Μά 'μεῖς δέν ἤλθαμε ἐδῶ νά φᾶ-, νά φᾶμε καί νά πιούμε,
μόνο σᾶς ἀγαπούσαμε, κ' ἤλθα-, κ' ἤλθαμε νά σᾶς δοῦμε.

Βγῆκα καί χαιρέτησα ὅλα τά ζευγαράκια·
τό πρῶτο πού χαιρέτησα ἦταν ' Ἅγιος Βασίλης.
5   —' Ἅγιε Βασίλη Δέσποτα, καλό ζευγάρι κάνεις.
—Μέ τήν εὐχή σ', ἀφέντη μου, καλό καί βλογημένο.
—Νά σέ ρωτήσω ἤθελα, πόσα πινάκια¹ σπέρνεις;
—Σιτάρι σπέρνω δώδεκα, κριθάρι δεκατρία·
κι αὐτά μοῦ τά ἐτρώγανε πέρδικες καί λαγούδια.
10 Καί θέρισα κι ἀνόλεψα ὅλα τ' ἀπεφαγούδια,
καί βγῆκαν χίλια μέτρητα καί χίλια μετρημένα.
Κ' ἐκεῖ πού τά λογάριαζα, νά, κι ὁ Χριστός κ' ἔπερνα,
κ' ἐκεῖ πού στάθηκε ὁ Χριστός, χρυσό δεντράκι βγῆκε·
στή μέση ἦταν ὁ σταυρός, στή μπάντα τά βαγγέλια,
15 καί κάτω στή ριζίτσα του, μιά βρύση κρυσταλένια.
Καί κατεβαῖναν πέρδικες κ' ἔβρεχαν τά φτερά τους,
κ' ἔλουζαν τόν ἀφέντη μας,
τό ρῆγα, τό λεβέντη μας, τόν πολυχρονεμέμος
καί στόυ κοσμό ξακουσμένος.

Παινέματα:
20 Μά σέ σοῦ πρέπ' ἀφέντη μου,
βρέ ρῆγα, βρέ λεβέντη μου, καρριόλα νά κοιμᾶσαι,
βελούδο νά σκεπάζεσαι νά μή κρυολογᾶσαι.
Πολλά 'παμε τ' ἀφέντη μας, ἄς ποῦμε τῆς κυρᾶς μας:
' Ἄν ἔχει κόρη ἔμορφη, γραμματικός τή θέλει·
25 ἄν εἶναι δέ γραμματικός, πολλά καλά γυρεύει·
γυρεύει τ' ἄσπρο² πρόβατο καί τό φεγγάρι γίδια,
τά κοχλιδάκια τοῦ γιαλοῦ γυρεύει δακτυλίδια.

Γιά δῶσε μας τόν πέτεινο
νά πᾶ' νά φύγομ' ἀπό δῶ, δῶς μας τήν ἄσπρη κόττα
30 γιά νά πᾶμε σ' ἄλλη πόρτα.

Καί τοῦ χρόνου.

¹ Πινάκια = μέτρον γεωργικό.
² 'Άστρο.

KALANDA FOR NEW YEAR'S

We didn't come here to eat and drink,
but only because we love you we came to see you.

I went out and greeted all the ploughing teams,
and the first one I greeted was Saint Vasili:
5   "Saint Vasili, Bishop, you've got a fine team."
"With your blessing, *afendi*, it's fine and blessed."
"I wanted to ask you something: how many bushels have you sown?"
"I've sown twelve of wheat, thirteen of barley,
but they were all eaten up by partridges and rabbits,
10   and I reaped the leftovers—
countless thousands, innumerable thousands.
And, there where I was counting them out, Christ passed by;
and, there where Christ stopped, a little golden tree came out.
At its mid-point was the cross; on the side the evangelists;
15   and down at its roots a crystal spring.
And partridges came down and sprinkled their wings
and washed our *afendi*,
our king and venerable *levendi*,
who is famous throughout the world."

Penemata:
20   It would become you, *afendi*,
king and *levendi*, a barrow to sleep in
and velvet to cover you so you don't catch cold.
We've said a lot for our *afendi*, let's sing to his lady:
if she's got a beautiful daughter, a clerk wants to marry her,
25   and, if he's a clerk, he's asking for a large dowry.
He's asking for the [star for] sheep and the moon for goats
and the shells of the seashore for rings.

Come give us the rooster
so we can leave from here, give us the white hen
30   so we can go to another door.

93. ΕΚΛΟΓΙΚΟ ΤΡΑΓΟΥΔΙ

Ἐκατερίνα Ζευγῶλα
Χ. Ἀπείρανθος, Νάξου

᾽Ηλ-θαν ἀπ' ὄ - λο τό νη-σί σή - μέ-ρα στό χω - ριό μας

Γύρισμα

Πρω-το - πα - πα - δά - κι, — γειά σου, Μέ τά

λε - βεν - το - παι - - δά σου.

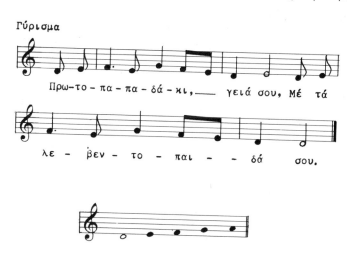

Ἦλθαν ἀπ' ὅλο τό νησί σήμερα στό χωριό μας
νά δοῦνε καί νά συγχαροῦν πάλι τόν ὑπουργό μας.

Εἶναι γεμάτο τό χωριό σήμερα μεγαλεῖω
γιατ' ἤτανε ἡ ἐκλογη σάν τό τριάντα-δύο.

5   Νά μᾶς ἐζήση ὑπουργος, ποτέ νά μή πεθάνη·
ἀλλά καί ζήτω τοῦ νησιοῦ καί πρῶτο τόν ἔβγανει.

Ἡ νίκη ἐξαιρετική ἔτανε τοῦ χωριοῦ μας
κι ἕνα στεφάνι δάφνινο πιάνει τοῦ ὑπουργο' μας.

<u>Γύρισμα:</u>
Πρωτοπαπαδάκι, γειά σου,
10 μέ τά λεβεντοπαιδά σου.

Ἡ νίκη ἐξαιρετική ἔτανε στό νησί μας
γιατί τόν ἐψηφίσανε ὅλοι οἱ δικοί μας.

Εἶναι ἡ δεκατή φορά αὐτή ἡ ἐκλογή σου
κι ὅλοι τή θαυμάζουνε τή τόση δυναμή σου.

15 Εἶναι ἡ δεκατή φορά πού στή Βουλή θά μπῆτε
καί μέ χωρίς συζήτηση γίνεται ὅτι πῆτε.

'Ενα τραγούδι θέ νά πῶ καί θέ νά τό φωνάξω:
ἐφέτη πάλι πήραμε ὁλόκληρη τή Νάξο.

Γιατί ἡ νίκη πάντοτε κοντά σου θέ νά μένη
20 κι ὅσο κι ἄν ἀγωνίζονται πάντοτε θἀν' χαμένοι.

Ἡπῆρε ὁ Καραμανλῆς τήν πλεονοψηφεία
καί διάλεο νᾶστε νά μπῆς πάλι στά ὑπουργεία.

Γειά σου, λεβέντη ὑπουργέ, γειά σου καί πάλι γειά σου.
Θέ νά γένης πρωθυπουργός πού 'τανε κι ὁ μπαμπᾶς σου.

25 Στρατό καί μηχανήματα ἤφερες στό νησί σου
καί ὅλοι οἱ αντίθετοι τά βάλανε μαζύ σου.

Στεφάνια σου προσφέρανε μέσ' στά χωριά τά ἄλλα
γιατί ὅλοι τά βλέπουνε τά ἔργα τά μεγάλα.

Πού δοξασμένο βρίσκεται πάντοτε τ' ὄνομά σου
30 καί τετραγωνικά μυαλά ἔχεις σά τό μπαμπᾶ σου.

<u>Γύρισμα:</u>
Εἶσαι ὑπουργός τριάντα
χρόνια καί θά βγαίνης πάντα.

ELECTION SONG

They've come to our village from all over the island today
to see and congratulate our deputy once again.

Our village is full of majesty today
because the election was like the one in '32.

5 Long live our deputy, never let him die,
and long live the island village where he came from.

This special victory belongs to our village,
and our deputy has caught a laurel wreath.

    Yirisma:
    Protopapadhaki, *yia sou*,
10   with your brave children.

This special victory belongs to our island
because all our own voted for him.

This is the tenth time, this election of yours,
and everyone marvels at your strength.

15 It's the tenth time that you'll enter Vouli
and, without debate, everything you say happens.

I want to sing a song and I want to shout it:
this year we took all of Naxos.

I want victory to stay with you always,
20 and, however much they struggle, they'll always be the losers.

Karamanlis took the majority vote,
and with him you'll always go into Vouli.

Yia sou, brave deputy, *yia sou*, and again *yia sou*,
I hope you become first deputy as your father did.

25 You brought roads and machines to our island,
and all your enemies have quarreled with you.

They're offering you crowns in the villages
because they all see your great works.

Your name will always be praised
30 and you've got a logical brain, just like your father.

    Yirisma:
    Thirty years a deputy,
    and you'll always win.

94. ΚΑΛΑΝΤΑ ΤΩΝ ΦΩΤΩΝ

Κωνσταντῖνος Κύτωης
Χ. Ἀπείρανθος, Νάξου

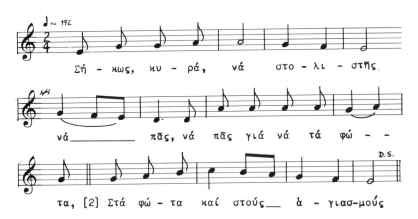

Σή - κως, κυ - ρά, νά στο - λι - στῆς.

νά_____ πᾶς, νά πᾶς γιά νά τά φώ - -

τα, [2] Στά φώ - τα καί στούς___ ἀ - γιασ-μούς

Σήκως, κυρά, νά στολιστῆς νά πᾶς, νά πᾶς γιά καί τά φώτα,

στά φώτα καί στούς ἀγιασμούς καί στίς χαρές τοῦ κόσμου.
Σηκώνεται, στολίζεται τρεῖς μέρες καί τρεῖς νύχτες·
βάζει τόν ἥλιο πρόσωπο καί τό φεγγάρ᾽ ἀχτιδι,[1]
5   καί τοῦ κοράκου τό φτερό βάζει κάτ᾽ ἀπ᾽ τό φρύδι.

[1] Τό φεγγάρι στῆθι (βλ. Passow, 222).

KALANDA FOR EPIPHANY

Get up, lady, get dressed and go to the Epiphany service,
the Epiphany service, the blessing of the water, the joys of the people.
She gets up and dresses herself for three days and three nights.
She puts on the sun for her face, the moon [for her breast],
5 and the wing of the raven she puts under her eyebrow.

95. Η ΒΛΑΧΑ

Κώστας Μαντζουράνης, Φρόσω
Μαντζουράνης, καί
Ἰωάννης Μαντζουράνης
Χ. Ἀπείρανθος, Νάξου (μαγνητοφώνησε
στή Χώρα)

Ψηλά τή χτίζεις τή φωλιά, (δίς)
  μά θά σοῦ γύρ' ὁ κλῶνος,
  κλῶνος, κλῶνος, μά θά σοῦ γύρ' ὁ κλῶνος,
μά θά σοῦ φύγη τό πουλί,

ἔτσι κι ἀμάν ἀμάνε,
βρέ, θά σοῦ μένη ὁ πόνος,
πόνος, πόνος, καί θά σοῦ μένη ὁ πόνος.

Τό κυπαρίσι τ᾽ ἀψηλο, ἀγέρας τό ζευλώνει·
τήν κοπελλιά τήν ἄγρια, ὁ νιός τήνε μερώνει.

5 Στό παραθύρι πούσαι ᾽σύ, γαρυφαλλιά δέν πρέπει
γιατ᾽ εἶσαι ᾽σύ γαρύφαλλιά κι ὁπόχει μάτια ἄς βλέπη.

SHEPHERD GIRL

You build your nest high up, but the branch will fly back on you,
the bird will leave you, and the pain will remain.

The wind yokes the tall cypress tree,
the youth tames the wild girl.

5 There's no need for a carnation at your window,
because you yourself are a carnation, and, whoever has eyes, let him
see it.

96. ΚΟΤΣΑΚΙΑ (' Ἔρι ἔρι)

Ἰωάννης Μαντζουράνης
Χ. Ἀπείρανθος, Νάξου (μαγνητοφώνησε
στή Χώρα)

'Ἔρι, ἔρι, ἔρι, ὄμορφο ὁποῦναι
ν' ἀγαπᾶ κανεῖς καί νά τόν ἀγαποῦνε.

'Ἔρι, ἔρι, ἔρι, ἡ μάνα του μέ βρίζει,
μά τό κοπελουδάκι μέ ὑποστηρίζει.

5   'Ἔρι, ἔρι, ἔρι, ἰάντα οἱ δικοί σου
δέν μ' ἀφήνουν νἄχω ἔρωτα μαζύ σου.

COUPLETS

Eri eri eri, how beautiful it is
to love and be loved.

Eri eri eri, her mother abuses me,
but the little girl supports me.

5 *Eri eri eri*, why won't your family
let me love you?

97. ΚΟΤΣΑΚΙΑ ΑΝΤΙΠΟΛΕΜΙΚΑ (Κοτσάτος)

Κώστας Μαντζουράνης καί
Φρόσω Μαντζουράνης
Χ. Ἀπείρανθος, Νάξου (μαγνητοφώνησε
στή Χώρα)

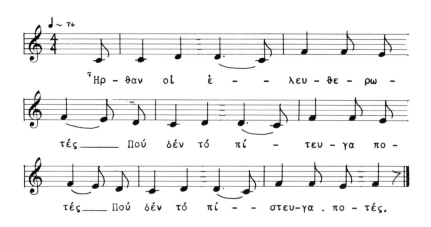

Ἦρθαν οἱ ἐλευτερωτές
πού δέν τό πίστευγα ποτές. (δίς)

Ἐγγλέσοι ἐλευθερωτές,
νά μήν πεθάνετε ποτές. (δίς)

5 Ἦρθαν οἱ Ἀμερικάνοι
καί κανείς δέν θά πεθάνη. (δίς)

WORLD WAR II COUPLETS

The liberators have come—
I thought they'd never come.

English liberators,
may you never die.

5   The Americans have come,
and no one is going to die.

98. Ο ΦΑΣΟΛΗΣ

Σαμσόν Λούκας, τραγούδι,
Ἰωάννης Ξανθάκης, βιολί,
καί Ἀποστάλεος Ἀβρανᾶς,
λαοῦτο.
Χ. Καταβατή, Σίφνου (μαγνητοφώνησε
στήν Ἀπόλλωνα)

Σ'ἔ-να σπι-τά-κι μέ-σα,

σ'ἔ-να σπι-τά-κι μέ-σα___ Σ'ἔ-
βιολί

να σπι-τά-κι μέ-σα___ μά δέν ἡ-ξέ-ρω πού.

Γύρισμα

Στήν___ καρ-διά, στήν___ καρ-διά,

Πέν-τε μῆ-νες, δυό___ παι-διά.

Βράχηκε ὁ Φασόλης, ἠβράχηκε ὁ Φασόλης,
ἠβράχηκε ὁ Φασόλης μέσα στό Χοντροποῦ

σ' ἕνα σπιτάκι μέσα, σ' ἕνα σπιτάκι μέσα,
σ' ἕνα σπιτάκι μέσα μά δέν ἠξέρω ποῦ.

Γύρισμα:
Στήν καρδιά, στήν καρδιά,
πέντε μῆνες, δυό παιδιά.

Τρία ψωμιά τοῦ πάω κ' ἕνα φλάκι κρασί
κι ἕνα βερούδι φάβα, ἴσως κι ἀνεπιαστεῖ.

(Γύρισμα)

5 Πάω κι ἄν δέν τόν εὑρῶ τό γέρο ζωντανό,
ἀπό κεῖ δά τήν πούντα θά πέσω νά πνίγω.

(Γύρισμα)
'Ω παραγυιέ, γιά πές μου, ὁ γέρος, τί ἔγινε;
τά μάτια μου τόν κλαῖνε κι ὁ νοῦς μου ἔμεινε.

FASOLIS

Fasolis was in danger from the rain and snow on Khondropou
    mountain
in a little hut, but I don't know where.

I'm taking him three loaves of bread and a flask of wine
and a box of fava beans; maybe he's recovered.

5 I'm going now, and if I don't find the old man alive
I'll throw myself down from the edge of Khondropou to drown.

Apprentice boy, tell me, what happened to the old man?
My eyes weep for him and my mind is confounded.

99. ΜΠΑΛΛΟΣ ΣΟΥΣΤΑ

Κώστας Πανώριος, τραγοῦδι καί
βιολί, Γιάννης Πανώριος,
λαοῦτο, καί Πέτρος Πανώριος, κιθάρα
Χ. Καρδιανή, Τήνου

'Αρ - με - να - κι   'μαι, κυ - ρά___ μου, πά - ρε
Ά - νοι - ξε   τις   δυό σ' ά - γκά - λες, βά - λε

με,   πά - ρε   μεν, δέν ντα - για - - ντῶ,
με,   βά - λε   με   νά   σέ   χά - - ρω.

Ἀρμενάκι 'μαι, κυρά μου, πάρε με, πάρε με, δέν νταγιαντῶ,[1]
ἄνοιξε τίς δύο σ' ἀγκάλες, βάλε με, βάλε με, νά σέ χάρω.

Τά καϋμένα τά πουλάκια, πῶς τό πίνουν τό νερό
πῶχει μέσα τό φαρμάκι τῆς ἀγάπης τόν καϋμό.

BALLOS SOUSTA DANCE

I'm a little ship, lady, take me, I can't stand it;
open your two arms and put me there so I can please you.

Poor birds, how can they drink that water
that's got in it the bitter sorrow of love?

[1] Νταγιαντῶ = ὑποφέρω (λ.τ. *dayanmak*).

100. ΤΑ ΜΑΓΙΑ

Κώστας Πανώριος, τραγούδι καί
βιολί, Γιάννης Πανώριος,
λαούτο, καί Πέτρος Πανώριος, κιθάρα
Χ. Καρδιανή, Τήνου

Γιά μά-για, μά-για__ μού-κα - νες, κα-λέ μου,
Καί στά ὠ - ραῖ-α__ σου μαλ - λιά, κα-λέ μου,

γιά μα - γευ-μέ - νο___ μέ - - χεις,
πε - ρι - πλεγ-μέ - νο___ μέ - - χεις.

Γύρισμα

Γιά μάγια, μάγια μοὔκανες, καλέ μου, γιά μαγευμένο μ' ἔχεις,
καί στά ὡραῖα σου μαλλιά, καλέ μου, περιπλεγμένο μ' ἔχεις.

Γύρισμα:
Γιά μαγευμένο μ' ἔχεις,
περιπλεγμένο μ' ἔχεις.

THE BEWITCHING

You've cast a spell over me, you've bewitched me,
and you've entangled me in your beautiful hair.

Yirisma:
You've bewitched me,
you've entangled me.

101. ΘΑ ΣΠΑΣΩ ΚΟΥΠΕΣ

Κώστας Πανώριος, τραγοῦδι καί
βιολί, Γιάννης Πανώριος,
λαοῦτο, καί Πέτρος Πανώριος, κιθάρα
Χ. Καρδιανή, Τήνου

θά σπά-σω κού - πες___ γιά τά λό-για ποῦ - πες

Καί πο - τη - ρά - κια γιά τά πε - ρι - γα - λά - κια.

"Ωχ, _____ ὤχ, δέν βγαί-νεις νά σέ ἰ - δῶ,

"Ωχ, _____ ὤχ,   νά   πα - ρη - γο - ρι - θῶ.

Θά σπάσω κούπες
γιά τά λόγια ποῦπες
καί ποτηράκια
γιά τά περιγαλάκια.
5   ''Ωχ, ὤχ, δέν βγαίνεις νά σέ ἰδῶ,
      ὤχ, ὤχ, νά παρηγοριθῶ.

Χθές τό βράδυ σ'εἶδα στ' ὄνειρό μου,
πώς εἶχες τά μαλλάκια σου ριγμένα στό λαιμό σου.
      ''Ωχ, ὤχ, δέν ξημερώνουμαι·
10   ὤχ, ὤχ, πώς φαρμακόνουμαι.

Χθές τό βράδυ
σ'εἶδα στό σκοτάδι,
σ'εἶδα πώς μιλοῦσες
καί μέ περιφρονοῦσες.
15   ''Ωχ, ὤχ, πάπια-χήνα μο',
      ὤχ, ὤχ, νἄχης τό κριμα μου.

Θά σπάσω κούπες
γιά τά λόγια ποῦπες
καί ποτηράκια
20   γιά τά κοριτσάκια.
      ''Ω, ὤχ, δέν βγαίνεις νά σέ ἰδῶ,
      ὤ, ὤχ, νά παρηγοριθῶ.

I'LL SMASH CUPS

I'll smash cups
for the words you said,
and glasses
for your blue, blue eyes.
5   Why don't you come out so I can see you,
so I can be consoled.

Last night I saw you in my dream,
and you had your hair thrown down over your throat.
I can't wake up;
10   oh, how I'm grieving!

Last night
I saw you in the dark,
I saw how you were talking:
you were treating me scornfully.
15   My little duck-goose,
you should pity me.

I'll smash cups
for the words you said,
and glasses
20   for the young girls.
Why don't you come so I can see you,
so I can be consoled.

102. ΤΟ ΜΠΑΡΜΠΟΥΝΑΚΙ (Συρτός)

Κώστας Πανώριος, τραγούδι
καί βιολί, Γιάννης Πανώριος,
λαοῦτο, καί Πέτρος Πανώριος, κιθάρα
Χ. Καρδιανή, Τήνου

... μπαρμπουνάκι μου, ἀμάν,
κι ὀλόχρυσό, κι ὀλόχρυσό μου ψάρι,

. . . .

Ἐγώ τραβῶ, ἐγώ τραβῶ τούς πόνους σου,
κι ὀλόχρυσό, κι ὀλόχρυσό μου ψάρι,
ἄλλος νά μή, ἄλλος νά μήν σέ πάρη.

LITTLE RED MULLET (*Syrtos* dance)

... my little red mullet, my golden fish,
I endure the pain you cause lest someone else take you away.

103. Η ΣΑΚΚΟΥΛΑ (Συρτός)

Κώστας Πανώριος, τραγούδι καί
βιολί, Γιάννης Πανώριος,
λαοῦτο, καί Πέτρος Πανώριος, κιθάρα
Χ. Καρδιανή, Τήνου

Εἶ - χα πέν-τε τά - λη - ρα καί τἄ - πα - ρα στή

πρέ - φα· Καί πα - ρᾶς δέν μοῦ- μει - νε νά

βιολί

πά - ρω μιά γυ - ναῖ - - κα.

Εἶχα πέντε τάληρα καί τἄπαρα στή πρέφα·
καί παρᾶς δέν μοὔμεινε νά πάρω μιά γυναῖκα.

Εἶχα πέντε τάληρα καί τἄπαιξα στό ζάρι·
καί παρᾶς δέν μοὔμενε νά πάρω ἕνα ζωνάρι.

5 Εἶχα πέντε τάληρα καί μιά ἀργεντινή[1]
κ᾿ ἔπαιξα καί γλέντησα γιά μιά μελαχροινή.

THE MONEY POUCH (*Syrtos* dance)

I had five *talira* and I took them to the card game,
and not a cent was left for me to take a wife with.

I had five *talira* and I gambled at backgammon,
and not a cent was left for me to buy a belt with.

5 I had five *talira* and an *arghendini*,
and I played and made merry with a brown-haired girl.

[1] Ἀργεντινή = πάλιο νόμισμα τῆς Ἀθῆνας.

104. ΜΠΑΛΛΟΣ ΜΑΣΤΙΧΑ

Πέτρος Πανώριος, τραγοῦδι καί
κιθάρα, Κώστας Πανώριος,
βιολί, καί Γιάννης Πανώριος, λαοῦτο
Χ. Καρδιανή, Τήνου

Ὁ ἥλιος βασιλεύει στά παραθύρια σου,
κ' ἐσύ, διαβολοκόρη, βάφεις τά φρύδια σου.

Ὁ ἥλιος βασιλεύει κ' ἡμέρα σώνεται,
κ' ἐμένα τό πουλί μοῦ δέν φανερώνεται.

5   Ἐσύ μ' αὐτή τή γνώμη κ' ἐγώ μ' αὐτό τό νοῦ·
νά δοῦμε ποιός θά πέση "συγγνώμη" τ' ἄλλονου.

MASTIC *BALLOS* DANCE

The sun is setting in your windows,
and you, devil-girl, you paint your eyebrows.

The sun is setting and day is ending,
and my little bird doesn't show herself to me.

5 You with your opinion, I with my own mind,
we'll see who says "excuse me" to the other.

105. ΜΠΑΛΛΟΣ

Πέτρος Πανώριος, τραγοῦδι καί
κιθάρα, Κώστας Πανώριος,
βιολί, καί Γιάννης Πανώριος, λαοῦτο
Χ. Καρδιανή, Τήνου

'Α - πο - φά - ση - σα _____ νά γί - νω στήν 'Α - γιά Σο-
Νἄρ-χον-τε νά προ - σκυ-νά-νε ἄ - σπρες καί με-

φιά κου-πές
λα - χροι-νές.

τραγοῦδι   βιολί

'Αποφάσησα νά γώω στήν 'Αγία Σοφιά κούπες
νἄρχοντε νά προσκυνάνε ἄσπρες καί μελαχροινές.

Σὰν τίς μαρμαροκολόνες στέκεις μέσ' στήν ἐκκλησιά,
καί μαραῖνεις καί τρελλαίνεις νέους, γέρους καί παιδιά.

BALLOS DANCE

I've decided to become the domes on Hagia Sofia
so white-skinned girls and brunettes can come and worship.

Like the marble columns, you stand in the church,
and you make youths, old men, and children languish and go crazy.

106. ΤΗΣ ΤΡΙΑΝΤΑΦΥΛΛΙΑΣ ΤΑ ΦΥΛΛΑ

'Αριστόδημος Ράμπιας, τραγοῦδι καί
λαοῦτο, καί Μιχαήλ Ράμπιας, σαντούρι
Μύκονος

"Ε̱, — τῆς τρι-αν-τα - - φυλ-λιᾶς τά___ φυλ-λα
σαντούρι
θά τά κά - - νω φο - ρε - σιά

Νά τά βάλ', νά πε-ρασ' ἐ-γώ,___ νά τά βά-λω,
σαντούρι
νά πε - ρά - σω νά σοῦ κά - ψω τήν καρ-διά.

'Έ, τῆς τριανταφυλλιᾶς τά φύλλα θά τά κάνω φορεσιά
νά τά βάλ', νά περάσ' ἐγώ, νά τά βάλω, νά περάσω,
νά σοῦ κάψω τήν καρδιά.

Κάν' τά μαλλιά σου, κάν' τα, κάν' τα σκάλες ν' ἀνεβῶ,
νά φιλήσω τήν ἐληά σου καί τόν ἄσπρο σου λαιμό.

5 'Από τά γλυκά σου μάτια βρέχ' τ' ἀθανατό νερό,
καί σοῦ ζήτησα λιγάκι καί δ έν μοῦδωσες νά πιῶ.

. . . .
. . . .

Μή μοῦ διπλοκαταριέσαι, θά πετάνω καί θά κλαῖς,
10 κ' ὕστερα θά μετανοιώσης, "κρῖμα τό παιδί" θά λές.

THE LEAVES OF THE ROSEBUSH

I'll make the leaves of the rosebush into a costume
and put them on to pass by, so I can burn your heart.

Fix your hair, fix it, make it into a ladder so I can climb up,
so I can kiss your beauty mark and your white neck.

5 From your sweet eyes runs the immortal water,
and I asked you for a little and you wouldn't give me any to drink.

. . . .
. . . .

Don't double-curse me. I'll die and then you'll cry.
10 Later you'll repent, "What a shame!" you'll say.

107. ΑΝΩ ΜΕΡΑ, ΚΑΛΟ ΧΩΡΙΟ

Ἀριστόδημος Ράμπιας, τραγοῦδι καί
λαοῦτο, καί Μιχαήλ Ράμπιας, σαντούρι
Μύκονος

Ἄνω Μερά, Ἄνω Μερά, καλό χωριό
καί μέ τίς πρασινάδες, καί μέ τίς πρασινάδες,

ἐγώ 'μαι πού, ἐγώ 'μαι πού σέ γλένταγα·
δέν ἔχω πιά παράδες, καί μέ τίς πρασινάδες.

'Αλλοί, καϋμέ, ἀλλοί, καϋμέ ' Ἄνω Μερά,
τά τέκνα σου ξορίζεις, τά τέκνα σου ξορίζεις,
τούς ξένους κά-, τούς ξένους κάνεις ἐδικούς
καί μᾶς, δέν μᾶς γνωρίζεις, καί μᾶς, δέν μᾶς γνωρίζεις.

5 'Αλλοί, καϋμέ, ἀλλοί καϋμέ ' Ἄνω Μερά,
πού θά τά πᾶς τά βούδια, πού θά τά πᾶς τά βούδια;
Νάρθῶ νά κου-, νάρθῶ νά κουβεντιάσωμε,
ἀγάπη μου καινούργια, πού θά τά πᾶς τά βούδια.

GOOD VILLAGE ANO MERA

Good village Ano Mera, with all the greenery,
I'm the one who feasted you; I haven't got any more money.

Ah, poor Ano Mera, you exile your children,
you adopt foreigners, and you don't recognize us.

5 Ah, poor Ano Mera, where are you taking the cows?
Let me come along so we can talk together, my new love.

108. ΚΑΛΑΝΤΑ ΤΗΣ ΠΡΩΤΟΧΡΟΝΙΑΣ

Βγενούλα Κουσαθανά
Μύκονος

' Άγης Βασιλης ἔρχεται ἀπό τήν Καισαρία.
Βαστᾶ εἰκόνα καί χαρτί, χαρτί καί καλαμάρι.
—Βασίλη μου, πόθεν ἔρχεσαι καί πόθεν κατεβαίνεις;
—'Από τῆς μάνας μ' ἔρχομαι καί στό σκολειό μου πάγω.
5   —Κά(τ)σε νά φᾶς, κά(τ)σε νά πιγῆς, κά(τ)σε νά τρα(γ)ουδήσης·
κι ἄν εἶσαι καί γραμματικός, πές μας τήν ἀλφαβῆτα.
Καί τό ραβδί το' ἀκούμπισε νά πῆ τήν ἀλφαβῆτα.
Καί τό ραβδί, χλουρό ραβδί, χλουρό βλαστάριο 'πητα·
κι ἀπάνω στά βλαστάρια του, μιγάδια καί πηγάδια,
10 μιγάδια πετροπήγαδα κι αὐλές μαρμαρομένες.

Νά κατεβαίνουν οἱ πέρδικες νά πίνουν ν' ἀνεβαίνουν,
νά βρέχουν κ'οἱ φτερούγες των, νά ραίνουν τόν ἀφέντη.

Παίνεμα:
'Αφέντη, ἀφέντη, ὀλάφεντε, πέντε φορές ἀφέντη,
ἐσένα πρέπει, ἀφέντη μου, βελούδια νά κομᾶσαι,
15 βελούδια νά σκεπάξεσαι νά μήν κρυολογᾶσαι.
Καί πάλι ξαναπρέπει σου τρικούβερτο καράβι·
ἡ πρύμη νᾶναι τό μάλαμα κ' ἡ πλώρη τό λογάρι,
καί τά σκοινιά τοῦ καραβιοῦ ὁλομαργαριτάρι.
Νά τά μαζεύου' οἱ ἄρχοντες νά κάνουνε δακτυλίδια,
20 καί τά μικρά ἀρχοντόπουλα νά κάνουν βουλωτήρια.

Γιά δ ῶσε μας τόν πετεινό, γιά δ ῶσε μας τήν κότα,
γιά δ ῶσε μας τήν πλερωμή νά πᾶμε σ' ἄλλη πόρτα.

Καί τοῦ χρόνου, καί τοῦ χρόνου ἀφεντικό.

KALANDA FOR NEW YEAR'S

Saint Vasili is coming from Caesaria,
carrying an ikon and paper, paper and inkwell.
"Vasili, where are you coming from and where are you descending
    from?"
"I'm coming from my mother's and I'm going to school."
5 "Sit down to eat, sit down to drink, sit down to sing,
and, if you're a grammarian, tell us the alphabet."
And he leaned on his stick to say the alphabet,
and the stick, a green stick, put forth green shoots.
And, on its branches, almonds and wells,
10 almonds, stonewells, and marble courtyards,
so the partridges can come down to drink and go up again,
so they can wash their wings and sprinkle our *afendi*.

Penema:
Afendi, afendi, all-*afendi,* five-times *afendi,*
it would become you to sleep on velvet, *afendi,*
15 to be covered with velvet so you don't catch cold.

And it would also become you to have a three-decked ship,
the stern to be of gold and the bow of treasure
and the ropes of the ship—all pearl,
so the nobles can gather them up to make rings
20   and the little nobles' sons to make marbles.

Come, give us the rooster, come, give us the hen,
come, give us our reward so we can go to another door.

109. ΚΑΛΑΝΤΑ ΤΗΣ ΠΡΩΤΟΧΡΟΝΙΑΣ

Βγενούλα Κουσαθανά
Μύκονος

Ἀρχιμηνιά κι ἀρχιχρονιά κι ἀρχῆς τοῦ Γενναρίου
κι ἀρχῆς ποὺ βγῆκεν ὁ Χριστός στή γῆ νά περπατήξη.
. . . .
Χρυσά 'τανε τά κλωνάρια του κι ὀλάργυρη ἡ κορφή του.
στή μέση κάθετ' ὁ Χριστός, στήν ἄρχαν Παναγία
5 κι στά ψηλά κλωνάρια του, ἄγγέλοι κι ἀρχάγγελοι.
Κι ὁ Μιχαήλ Ἀρχάγγελος ἐπέρασεν καί λέει:
—Χαρίσετέ μου τά κλειδιά καί τά μαλαματένια
ν' ἀνοίξω τήν Παράδεισο νά πιῶ νερό δροσάτο,
νά πέσω ν' ἀποκοιμηθῶ σέ μιά μηλεά 'πό κάτω,
10 νά πέσουν τ' ἄνθ' ἀπάνω μου, τά ρόδα στήν ποδιά μου
καί τά χρυσά τριαντάφυλλα στήν ροδοπλεξουδιά μου.

Παύεμα:
Ν' ἔχεις τό γυιό, τόν καλογυιό, τό μοσκοκακνακάρι,
λούζεις τον καί χτενίζεις τον καί στό σκολειό τόν παίρ'εις.
Κι ὁ δάσκαλος τόν ἤβαλε γιά νά καλοαρχίση.
15 Κι ἐξέφυγεν του τό κερί κι ἤκαψεν τό χαρτί του.
Καί μάλαξεν τά ροῦχα του, τά μοσκοκεντημένα,
ὅπου τοῦ τά κεντούσανε οἱ τρεῖς βασιλιοπούλες:
ἡ μιά 'τανε τοῦ πρίτζηπα καί ἡ ἄλλη τοῦ βηζίρη
κ' ἡ ἄλλη πιό μικρότερη ἦταν τοῦ βασιλέα.

20 Κι ἐξεβοΐσαν τό κερί, ἀνέβα καί κατέβα,
καί κά(τ)σε καί λογάριασε ἤντα θά μᾶς ἐδόσης:
γιά πῆτα, γιά λουκάνικο, γιά καφτερή κομμάτι,
γιά ἀπό τῆ' μάνας τό πουγκί κανένα 'κοσαράκι,
γιά ἀπό τ' ἀφέντης τή πούζου κανένα διφραγγάκι.

Καί τοῦ χρόνου, καί τοῦ χρόνου νᾶστε καλά.

KALANDA FOR NEW YEAR'S

The month's beginning, the year's beginning and the beginning of
    January,
the beginning of the time when Christ came out to walk on earth.
. . . .
Its branches were golden, its summit all silver.
Christ is sitting in the middle, the Virgin at the top,
5 and on its high branches angels and archangels.
And the Archangel Michael passed by and speaks:
"Give me the golden keys
so I can open up Paradise and drink cool water,
so I can go to sleep under an apple tree,
10 so the blossoms will fall on me, the roses in my lap,
and the golden roses on my rose braid."

Penema:
If you've got a son, a good son, a musk son,
wash him and comb him and send him to school.
And the teacher set him to make a good beginning
15 and his candle fell and burned his paper.
And he rubbed his clothes, the musk-embroidered ones,
the ones that were embroidered for him by three princesses:
the one was a prince's daughter, the other a vizier's,
and the other, the youngest one, was a king's daughter.

20 The candle is finished, go up and go down
and sit down and count up whatever you're going to give us:
pie or sausage or a piece of something hot
or a twenty-lepta piece from the mother's purse
or a two-drachma piece from the *afendi*'s pocket.

110. ΚΑΛΑΝΤΑ ΤΗΣ ΠΡΩΤΟΧΡΟΝΙΑΣ (Τά σκυλομούλαρα)

Βγενούλα Κουσαθανᾶ
Μύκονος

Ἀνέβαινα, κατέβαινα τ᾽ ᾽ Ἀη Γιωργιοῦ τή σκάλα.
Χρυσό πουλάκι ἀμπάντηξα, σταυρό καί δακτυλίδι·
καί στήν πούξου μου τὄβαλα, στή μάνα μου τό πάω.
—Μάνα κι ἄν εἶσαι μάνα μου κ᾽ ἐγώ παιδέ δικό σου,
5 κάνε θερμό καί λοῦσε με μέ τσ᾽ ἀργυρολέγενες,
καί βάλε μου τή σκούφια μου, τήν τρανταμασουρένια,
πὤχει τά ν-τρανταμάσουρα, τά ν-τρανταμασουρούδια,
πὤχει δυό κοῦπες μέ ἄνθο, δυό κοῦπες μέ λουλούδια.
Λουλούδια, λουλουδάκια μου, πετάξετέ με πέρα
10 νά διῶ τό θειό μου ρόδινο, τόν κύρι μου φεγγάρι,
νά δῶ τόν πρῶτο μ᾽ ἀδερφό στή μούλα καβαλλάρη,
Νά πέφτουνε τά ταμπούρα του, νά πέφτη τό λογάρι.
᾽ Ἐλάτε, χῆρες κι ἄναντρες, μαζεύετε λογάρι·
νά πάρω ἐγώ τά πίτερα κ᾽ ἐσεῖς τό σιμιγδάλι.

15 ᾽ Ἅγιος Βασίλης κάθεται ἀπάνω στό βουνάλι·
βλέπει τά σκυλομούλαρα πού κάνουν τό ζευγάρι.
—᾽ Ἅγιε Βασίλη μου, Δέσποτα, πόσο κριθάρι σπέρνεις;
—Σπέρνω κριθάρι δ ώδεκα, νιγάδι δεκατρία,
σπέρνω καί ρόβω τέσσαρα κι ἀπονωρίς στό στάβλο.
20 ᾽ Ἤμαθα πώς τά φάγανε λάγοι καί περδικάκια·
καί θέρισα καί ᾽ποθέρισα ὅλα τ᾽ ἀπαφαγάκια.
Κ᾽ ἤκαμα χίλια μετρητά καί χίλια μετρημένα.
Τήν ὥρα πού τά μέτρουμε, νά, κι ὁ Χριστός καί κ᾽ ἐπερνάει.
Κ᾽ ἤσκυψεν καί τά βλόησε μέ τή δεξιά του χέρα,
25 μέ τή δεξιά, μέ τή ζερβιά, μέ τή μαλαματένια.
(Κ᾽ ἤκαμα χίλια μετρητά καί χίλια μετρημένα.)

Κι ἄν ἔ(χ)ης κίτρο, κόψε το, δῶς μας το μέ τό μέλι,
γιατ᾽ εἴμαστα ἀπ᾽ τά κάλαντα κ᾽ εἴμαστα βραχνιασμένοι.
Κι ἄν ἔχης κόρη ἔμορφη, βάλ᾽ την νά μᾶς κεράση,
30 νά τή φχηθοῦμε ὅλοι μας νά ζῆ καί νά γεράση.

Κι ἄν ἔχης καί γυιό στά γράμματα, νά σύρη τό κοντώλι,
νά τοῦ φχηϑοῦμε ὅλοι μας νά βάλη πετραχῆλι.

Καί τοῦ χρόνου καί καλή χρονιά.

KALANDA FOR NEW YEAR'S (The "dogs-and-mules" kalanda)

I was going up and down Saint George's ladder,
and I came across a golden bird, a cross, and a ring;
I put it [?] in my pocket and took it to my mother.
"Mother, if you are my mother and I am your son,
5   warm up some water and wash me with silver coins [?]
and put my thirty-times-gathered cap on me,
the one that's got thirty gathers on it,
the one that's got two crowns with blossoms, two crowns with
     flowers."
Flowers, little flowers, throw me away over there
10 so I can see my rose-colored uncle, my lord the moon,
so I can see my eldest brother riding a mule.
Let his tambourines fall down, let the treasure fall down.
Come widows and husbandless women, gather up the treasure.
Let me take the wheat husks, and you the wheat grain.

15 Saint Vasili is sitting on top of the mountain
looking at the teams of dogs and mules.
"Saint Vasili, Bishop, how many measures of oats have you planted?"
"I've planted twelve of oats, thirteen of a mixture,
four of tobacco and back to the stable by early evening.
20 And I discovered that the rabbits and partridges ate them all up,
and I reaped all the leftovers:
countless thousands, innumerable thousands.
And, just when we were counting them, Christ passed by,
and he bent over and blessed them with his right hand,
25 with his right hand, with his left hand, with his gold hand."
(Countless thousands, innumerable thousands.)

If you've got any citron, cut it and give it to us with honey
because we're hoarse from singing the kalanda.

And, if you've got a beautiful daughter, let her treat us something
30 so we can all wish her a long life.
And, if you've got a son learning his letters, let him write something
with chalk
so we can all wish him a priest's life.

NOTES TO THE SONGS

Abbreviations Used in Notes

Baud-Bovy, *Cleftique*   S. Baud-Bovy, *Etude sur la chanson cleftique avec 17 chansons cleftiques de Roumélie transcrites d'après les disques des Archives Musicales de Folklore.*

Baud-Bovy I or II   S. Baud-Bovy, Τραγούδια τῶν Δωδεκανῆσων, Vol. I or II.

EDT I   G.K. Spyridakis, G.A. Megas, and Dh. Petropoulos, Ἑλληνικά δημοτικά τραγούδια: 'εκλογή, Vol. I.

EDT III   G.K. Spyridakis and Spyros Peristeris, Ἑλληνικά δημοτικά τραγούδια: μουσική 'εκλογή, Vol. III.

Fauriel   Claude Fauriel, Δημοτικά τραγούδια τῆς συγχρόνου Ἑλλάδα.

IDT   Athanasios Yiagas, Ἠπειρωτικά δημοτικά τραγούδια.

Instruments   G.K. Spyridakis et al., '' Εκθεσες Ἑλληνικῶν λαϊκῶν μουσικῶν ὀργάνων/ *Exposition d'Instruments de musique populaires grecs.*

Megas   G.A. Megas, *Greek Calendar Customs.*

Merlier   Melpo Merlier, Τραγούδια τῆς Ρούμελης.

Pakhtikos   G. Pakhtikos, 260 δημώδη Ἑλληνικά 'ασματα.

Passow   Arnoldus Passow, Τραγούδια Ρωμάικα: *Popularia Carmina Graeciae Recentioris.*

Politis   N. Politis, Ἐκλογαί ἀπό τά τραγούδια τοῦ Ἑλληνικόῦ λάου.

NOTES TO THE SONGS

(A roman numeral followed by an arabic number indicates the tape number and song number in my collection. Most of the variants are of the Greek lyrics only; those which are of the tune as well are noted. The ages of the singers, which follow their names in parentheses, are approximate. In the pitches indicated, *c'* = middle c.)

THE PELOPONNESOS

TRIPOLIS is the capital of the province of Arkadhia in the central Peloponnesos. The following song was recorded in the informant's home there on April 2, 1964.

Song 1. Ὁ Ἀμάραντος / *The Amaranth*
(XVI, 7. Original tonic: *c#'-e'.*)
Singer: Konstandinos Broutzas (16).
Variant: *EDT* III, 346. An English translation of another variant appears in Hilary Pym, *Songs of Greece,* 51.

VYTINA is a large village about twenty miles northwest of Tripolis. The Stavropoulos family all sang, from old Barba-Yioryios (who had spent 40 of his 80 years in America, yet knew many *kleftic* songs), down to the triplet boys who sang *Song 4* below. The songs were recorded in the Stavropoulos home on April 1, 1964.

Song 2. Περδικούλα τοῦ Μωρέα / *Little Partridge of Morea*
(XVI, 10. Original tonic: *f.*)
Singer: Aryirios Stavropoulos (35).
Line 1. Morea, the popular name for the Peloponnesos.
Line 3. Theodhoros Kolokotronis (1770-1843), famous *kleft* captain of the Peloponnesos and hero of the Greek War of Independence.
Line 5. Tsaldi, a legendary Robin Hood-like figure. His "tree" (where supposedly his treasure is buried) and his "plaque" stood until the beginning of this century. (I am indebted to an unnamed reader for the American Folklore Society for this information.)

Song 3. Οἱ Κολοκοτρωναῖοι / *The Kolokotronis Band of "Klefts"*

(XVI, 11. Original tonic: *f#*.)
Singer: Aryirios Stavropoulos (35).
Variant: Baud-Bovy, *Cleftique*, 66-68; *EDT* III, 71-72 (text and music).
Line 2. Arkoudhorema (Bear ravine) and Limbovisi, both former villages of Arkadhia and both now in ruins. The former was the birthplace of Kolokotronis' grandfather, and the latter the birthplace of his father.

Song 4. Σιγαλά βρέχει ὸ οὺρανός / *Softly the Rain Falls*
(XVI, 17. Original tonic: *e '*.)
Singers: Ghrighorious, Vasilios, and Khrisostomos Stavropoulos (9).
Variant: XVI, 1, collected in Tripolis.

KALAMATA is the capital of the province of Messinia in the southern Peloponnesos. The following song was recorded in the informant's home on the outskirts of Kalamata on April 5, 1964.

Song 5. Κάλαντα τῶν φώτων / *"Kalanda" for Epiphany*
(XVII, 17. Original tonic: *g#*.)
Singer: Evangelia Panadelia (50).
Variants: Passow, 218; *EDT* III, 172-173.
The variant in Passow is closer to the Biblical version of the baptism of Christ: "Our Lord comes to the spring / and asks Saint John: / 'Great John the Baptist, / come baptize God's child.' / 'How can I? I can't / baptize you [who are] from heaven.' "

XYROKAMBI is a small village outside Sparti, in the district of Lakonia. Yioryios Dhoukas, a local schoolteacher, plays the bouzouki and sings popular music as well as folksongs. The following song was recorded in his home on April 14, 1964.

Song 6. Μάζευ' τά περιστέρια σου, κυρά μου / *Round up Your Pigeons, Lady*

(XIX, 15. Original tonic: *B* [voice] and *b* [*bouzouki*].)
Singer: Yioryios Dhoukas (45).

KATO PANAYIA is a tiny village in the northwest corner of the Peloponnesos, a few miles inland from the Ionian Sea. The citizens of the village originally came from a coastal village (also called Kato Panayia) of Asia Minor and were part of the massive Greek-Turkish population exchange of 1923. *Songs 7-9* and *13* are part of the Asia Minor tradition. The songs were recorded in the Fotaki and Zarghana homes, May 1-4, 1964.

Song 7. Ἡ Κλῶσσα / *The Broody Hen*

(XVII, 17. Original tonic: *d* '.)
Singer: Angelia Fotaki (55).
Variant: Baud-Bovy I, 31-33 (text and music).
Mrs. Fotaki repeated strophes 1 and 2 after she finished strophe 3.

Song 8. Κόκκινα μαντερινάκια / *Little Red Tangerines*
(XVII, 3. Original tonic: *e* '.)
Singer: Niki Dhouvitsa (20).
Mrs. Fotaki was teaching her niece, Niki Dhouvitsa, her entire repertory; she insisted that Niki sing this one alone. Niki did not know the
song well, and she extended it by repeating strophes 2 and 3. She also
tried, unsuccessfully, to fit the following distich to the melody:

'Ήθελα νά είχα δυό καρδιές, τήν μιά νά σοῦ χαρίσω,
τήν ἄλλη νά κρατῶ ἐγώ νά μή σ' ἀλησμονίσω.

I needed two hearts: one to give to you,
   and the other to keep myself so as not to forget you.

Mrs. Fotaki added a strophe in Turkish, between strophes 2 and 3
transcribed here.

Song 9. Μπάλλος / *Ballos Dance*
(XVIII, 2. Original tonic: *b* ♭.)
Singer: Angelia Fotaki (55).
Variant: Pernot, *Melodies populaires greques de l'île de Chio*, 39
(melody only).
Line 1. "They" are the musicians who, while they play the dance
music, sing complimentary distiches appropriate to the individual
dancers (such as the distich of lines 6-7).
Line 2. What I have translated as "find" is actually "search out," i.e.,
the musicians will go through their repertory of formulaic distiches to
find the ones that best fit the dancers.
Lines 3-5. Compare *Song 82.* Also compare the melodies.
For the *yirismata* sung on *la la la*, etc., Mrs. Fotaki used her voice like
an instrument, singing a decorated variant of the transcribed *yirisma*
melody.

Song 10. Κρητικιά μου λεμονιά / *My Cretan Lemon Tree*
(XVII, 9. Original tonic: *e* ♭ '.)
Singers: Angelia Fotaki (55) and Niki Dhouvitsa (20).
Mrs. Fotaki learned this song in Crete while visiting relatives there.
Lines 6, 10. Khania, a port in northwestern Crete.
Lines 7, 11. Iraklion (Candia), a port on the northern coast of Crete.
Line 10. Soudha, the name of the harbor at Khania.

Song 11. Μῆ μέ στέλνης, μάνα, στήν Ἀμερική / *Mother, Please Don't Send Me to America*
(XVII, 23. Original tonic: *b.*)
Singer: Aryiro Aravandinou (30).
Variant: XIV, 25, collected in Kalamata.

Song 12. Μοιρολόγι πρός τόν Βενιζέλον / *Lament for Venizelos*
(XVII, 15. Original tonic: *c'.*)
Singer: Gharifalia Souri (35).
The melody of this song was highly improvised. The second lines of strophes 2 and 3 are close to the music transcribed from the first strophe, but the first lines of these strophes and both lines of strophe 4 resemble the melody only in general contour.
Line 2. Eleftherios Venizelos (1864-1936), Cretan statesman and prime minister of Greece several times between 1924 and 1933.

Song 13. Μοιρολόγι τῆς Παναγίας / *The Virgin's Lament*
(XVIII, 6. Original tonic: *c#'.*)
Singers: Kaliopi Zarghana (55), Maria Minioti (45), Dina Maniati (25), Athana Kamenou (45), and Angelia Fotaki (55).
Variants: Passow, 230-232; *EDT* III, 188-191.
The text presented here is only about a third of the entire lament, as I ran out of tape while recording it. The variant given in *EDT* III is also from Asia Minor and is, in its first 32 lines, nearly identical with this one. It continues:

The women go to the house of the gypsy blacksmith who is making the nails for the crucifixion. He tells them that only four were ordered, but that he is making five: "two for his knees, two for his hands / and the other one, poisoned, [to go] deep into his heart . . ."

The Virgin faints again, is revived, and sets a curse on the gypsy: ". . . may you never succeed / nor have bread in your basket / nor clothes on your back / nor ashes on your hearth / and if one time you do, may the wind scatter them."

The Virgin then goes to Pilate's house where the door is tightly bolted. She commands the door to open, and it swings open from fear. Through it, she sees a multitude of people, including Saint John. She asks him where Christ is, and he points to the cross.

The Virgin approaches the cross and asks it to turn so that she can kiss her "little boy." From the cross Christ tells her to go home and spread a table with a black tablecloth and put wine in the water jug and wait until midnight Saturday night.

The Virgin follows his instructions and is mocked, first by Saint Kali and then by Bitter Laurel (she puts a curse on both of them). At midnight on Saturday, the heavens open and she sees Christ shining like a torch.

The recording session preceded by several days the ceremony that accompanies this lament. During the Maundy Thursday service, the Passion is read and a large wooden crucifix is set up in the middle of the church. After the service (well past midnight), the men and boys leave the church and the women and girls take positions around the cross, some kneeling, some standing. There they keep watch, singing the Virgin's lament and other popular hymns and songs, until dawn. (See Megas, 87-110, for a description of Easter week activities.)

EPIROS

METSOVON is a large, prosperous village set in the high mountain pass that connects Thessaly and Epiros. The villagers are bilingual, speaking Greek and the Vlach dialect common in many parts of mainland Greece.

The Pospotiki women (informants for *Songs 14-21*) are *sinnefadhes*, i.e., wives of two brothers, and the two families shared the same house. (Both families have since moved to Yiannina.) Like the other women of Metsovon, they wore the traditional village costume of long black skirts with embroidered aprons, bodices over embroidered blouses, and long scarves flowing down their backs. The songs were recorded in the Pospotiki home on September 4, 1964.

Yioryios Tsetsos (informant for *Songs 22-25*) was old and almost blind. He was the butt of the boys and young men of Metsovon, who considered him to be crazy. (The local story was that as a child he had been carried off by *klefts* and dropped on his head; Barba-Yioryios himself claimed that he had once been a *tselingas* (chief shepherd) with authority over 5,000 head of sheep.) The songs were recorded under the plane tree in the village square on July 23, 1967.

Song 14. Αὐτά εἶναι τά μάτια, Δῆμο μ', τἄμορφα / *These are the Beautiful Eyes, Dhimo*

(X, 14. Original tonic: *e'*.)

Singers: Marighoula Pospotiki (30) and Athanasia Pospotiki (25).

Variants: Fauriel, 248; Passow, 475; *EDT* III, 271-273; G.F. Abbott, *Macedonian Folklore*, 153.

Fauriel suggests that the song might have originally had historical significance, the "nine villages and ten *vilayets*" being definite villages and districts of *kleftic* jurisprudence, and Dhimos a particular *kleft* captain. His version has an additional strophe (between strophes 1 and 2):

Αὐτά μέ κάνουν, Δῆμο, κ᾽ ἀρρωστῶ,
Μέ κάνουν κ᾽ ἀπαιϑάινω.

They make me sick, Dhimo,
They make me die.

In one of the variants in *EDT* III, it is her husband rather than herself that the young woman asks Dhimo (her lover) to kill.

Song 15. Ὁ Μενούσης / *Menousis*
(X, 11. Original tonic: *c*ʹ.)
Singer: Marighoula Pospotiki (30).
Variants: *EDT* I, 374; Fauriel, 241-242; *IDT*, 287; Pakhtikos, 206-207; Passow, 341-342.

Song 16. Πέντε μῆνες περπατοῦσα / *Five Months I Roamed*
(X, 15. Original tonic: *e* ♭ ʹ.)
Singers: Marighoula Pospotiki (30) and Athanasia Pospotiki (25).
Variant: *IDT*, 315.

Song 17. Σαράντα-πέντε Κυριακές / *Forty-five Sundays*
(X, 12. Original tonic: *b*.)
Singers: Marighoula Pospotiki (30) and Athanasia Pospotiki (25).
Variants: *EDT* III, 216-217 (text and music); *IDT*, 333.
Lines 5-7. See *Songs 32* and *42*.
Line 6, in the Greek, is incomplete and the meter is faulty. Following the *tsakismata*-and-repetition pattern of the song, the singers began this half-line as the second part of the melodic strophe and should have repeated it, with the rest of the line, for the first part of the new musical strophe; instead they skipped directly into line 7. In other songs, the line is

Ποῦ ἤσουν ἐψές, λεβέντη μου, ποῦ ἤσουν προψές τό βράδυ;

but this formula was not available, since it is the boy speaking instead of the girl.

Song 18. Θέλησα νά κάνω γιούργια / *I Wanted to Attack*
(X, 13. Original tonic: *b*.)
Singer: Marighoula Pospotiki (30).

Song 19. Πέρα σ᾽ ἐκεῖο τό βουνό / *Over There on That Mountain*
(X, 10. Original tonic: *b* ♭ .)
Singer: Marighoula Pospotiki (30).
Variants: *EDT* III, 218-221 (text and music); Merlier, 42; XV, 11, collected in Thessaly.

Line 7, in the Greek, is incomplete and the meter is faulty, for the same reason as in *Song 17* above. In other variants the complete line is

Πῶς νά σ'κωθῶ, λεβέντη μου, ἀπό τήν ἀγκαλιά σου;

Song 20. Κόρη πού πᾶς στόν πόταμο / *When You Go to the River*
(X, 17. Original tonic: *c*#'.)
Singers: Marighoula Pospotiki (30) and Athanasia Pospotiki (25).
Variants: III, 3, collected in Rhodes; XIV, 9, collected in Macedonia.

Song 21. Κάλαντα τῶν Χριστουγέννων / *"Kalanda" for Christmas*
(XXII, 15. Original tonic: *e* ♭ '.)
Singer: Marighoula Pospotiki (30).
Line 4. Mrs. Pospotiki actually sang *"with the lemons are being squeezed* because Christ is born" (see the Greek text and footnote). My "correction" is from *IDT*, 203.
Lines 9-13. This *yirisma* is a linguistic hodgepodge. Mrs. Pospotiki insisted that it was in the Vlach dialect but, although she spoke that dialect fluently, she could elucidate only those phrases which are obviously Greek-derived (see Greek text and footnotes). Throughout Epiros *kalanda* are also known as *kolinda*, and many Epirotic *kalanda* begin: "*Kolinda, melinda . . .*" (See *IDT*, 201.)

Song 22. Βασιλαρχόντισσα / *Vasilo, the Arkhondissa*
(XII, 1. Original tonic: *g*.)
Singer: Yioryios Tsetsos (65).
Variant: *EDT* I, 302.
This song is about an abduction that took place in Metsovon in July of 1884. A village youth named Fleghas was struck by Metsovon notable Nikolas Averof for passing too close in front of the patricians of the village as they sat in front of the village church. Fleghas revenged himself by joining forces with Thimios Ghakis, a *kleft* captain in the district, to abduct Averof's daughter Evdhokia (changed to Vasilo in the song) and hold her for ransom. (*EDT* I, 302.)
Line 1. The first half of this line is a common formula. See Passow, 501, for several distiches that begin with it.
Line 5, in the Greek, has an extra syllable.
Line 7. Nikolanitsa, the feminine diminutive of Nikolas, here means "Nikolas' daughter."
I was unable to transcribe the last line and a half of the Greek text.

Song 23. Ἡ Περιστερούλα / *Peristeroula*
(XII, 11. Original tonic: *f*#.)
Singer: Yioryios Tsetsos (65).

This song came toward the end of the Sunday-afternoon recording session, by which time a large crowd had gathered to listen and comment. A few of the boys and young men were playing out their role of *pallikaria* by jeering and, in spite of efforts of the others to control them, they succeeded in confusing "Barba" Yioryios. Thus, the *tsamikos* meter does not emerge until the second musical strophe.

Line 1. The name Peristeroula means "little dove."

Song 24. Ἡ Βαγγελίτσα / *Vangelitsa*
(XII, 8. Original tonic: *f♯*.)
Singer: Yioryios Tsetsos (65).
Variant: XIV, 7, collected in Macedonia.

Song 25. Ὁ Πνευματικός / *The Confessor*
(XII, 6. Original tonic: *e♭*.)
Singer: Yioryios Tsetsos (65).
Variants: Baud-Bovy I, 110-111 (text and music); G. Kazavis, Νισύρου Λαογραφικά, 61; A. Thumb, *A Handbook of the Modern Greek Language*, 224.

Line 8. Literally, "you must not 'catch' love anymore."

Line 10. The "holy bread" is not communion bread (ἀντίδερο) but rather a round loaf that is blessed by the priest and cut up and distributed to the people after the service each Sunday.

ZITSA, a small village a few miles north of the city of Yiannina, is famous for its wine and its monastery (Profiti Ilias) where Lord Byron once stayed. The following song was recorded in the village schoolhouse on September 7, 1964.

Song 26. Κάλαντα τοῦ Λαζάρου / *"Kalanda" for Lazarus Day*
(XXII, 12. Original tonic: *f♯'*.)
Singers: Evangelos Tozolos, Dhimitrios Ghatsos, Paraskevi Exartou, Eleftheria Stamouli, and Evdhokia Papa (all elementary-school age).
Variant: *IDT*, 204.

The variant in *IDT* is identified as a Christmas *kalanda*, and the prayer is for the new-born baby: "May *he* become a king . . ." etc.

Line 8 is a common formulaic first line. In EDT I, 192, it begins a *kleftic* song ("The plains thirst for water and the mountains for snow / the hawks for chickens and the Turks for heads"); in *IDT*, 467, it is used for the opening of a bridal song ("The plains thirst for water and the mountains for snow / the hawk for wild olives and I, *kori*, for you").

MONODHENDRI is a small stone village in the Zaghori mountain range northeast of Yiannina. There are forty-six Zaghori villages scattered over the mountains, connected by dirt roads, footpaths, and in one case a long stone switchback stairway. Cutting through the Zaghori is the 3000-foot-deep Vikos gorge that runs northward toward Albania. The Monodhendri monastery (Roghovos cloister) hangs over the edge of this spectacular gorge.

Citizens of the Zaghori villages come from two very different socio-economic backgrounds: (1) the well-to-do merchant class whose money was traditionally earned abroad (in Roumania or any of the capitals of the Ottoman Empire); or (2) the Sarakatsani shepherds, a seminomadic community that uses the pastures of the Zaghori for summer grazing. (See John K. Campbell, *Honour, Family and Patronage*, 11-16.)

Kaliopi Ikonomidhou is an educated woman who taught school in Yiannina for many years before returning to her native village. The songs were recorded in her home on July 27, 1967.

Song 27. Μέ γέλασαν τά πουλιά / *The Birds Laughed at Me*
(XII, 11. Original tonic: *c#ʹ*.)
Singer: Kaliopi Ikonomidhou (50).
Variant: *EDT* III, 351-352.
The *yirismata* are not included in the line count in the Greek text.

Song 28. Ή γριά Τζαβέλινα / *Old Tzavelina*
(XII, 12. Original tonic: *b♭*.)
Singer: Kaliopi Ikonomidhou (50).
Variants: Baud-Bovy, *Cleftique*, 58-59 and 70-72; *IDT*, 133.
The second musical strophe begins with the second half of line 2.

Line 1. Souli, a group of villages in the wild and inaccessible Thesprotian mountains east of Yiannina, was an autonomous district during the eighteenth century. While other Greek villages were forced to pay taxes to the Ottoman oppressors, Souliotes maintained their independence and actually exacted tribute from both Greek and Turkish villages on the plains below. They were finally subdued (and almost totally annihilated) by Ali Pasha in a long series of campaigns beginning in 1792. (See William Plomer, *Ali the Lion*, 58 ff.)

Line 4. Tzavelina is the feminine form of Tzavelas, a family that included several Souliote heroes. She is Moskho, wife of Lambros Tzavelas, who, like many Souliote women, fought alongside the men in their desperate attempt to repel the invaders.

VITSA is another of the Zaghori villages, a few miles east of Monodhendri. Ioannis Roudas is a Sarakatsanos shepherd. The songs were recorded in front of the coffeehouse in Vitsa on July 28, 1967.

Song 29. Τοῦ Χατζημιχαήλ οἱ ἀνιψά / *Khatzimikhail's Nephews*

(XIII, 2. Original tonic: *f#*.)
Singer: Ioannis Roudas (50).
Line 1. Khatzimikhail is perhaps Khatzimikhalis Dalianis (1775-1828), an Epirote *kleft* captain from Dhelvinaki.
Line 3. Women's costumes in many parts of Greece include chains and necklaces made of old coins.
Line 4. Many *klefts*, especially the younger undisciplined men, were not above terrorizing their own compatriots. In his memoirs, Makriyannis describes an incident in which a group of *klefts*, while robbing a young Greek woman, were about to cut off her finger because her ring wouldn't slide off, but were finally persuaded to break the ring fastening instead. (See Makriyannis, *The Memoirs of General Makriyannis*, 39.)

Song 30. Ὁ Γιάκας / *Yiakas*
(XIII, 3. Original tonic: *b♭*.)
Singer: Ioannis Roudas (50).
Variants: *EDT* I, 258; *EDT* III, 73-74 (text and music; the tune is in 6/4 time); Pakhtikos, 313-314 (text and music; the tune is in 4/4 time); also *EDT* I, 179, in which the place names are changed to commemorate a battle of 1912.
Yiakas is a corruption of Ziakas (Theodhoros) who was an *armatoli* from the Makrynorous mountains of Ghrevena in western Macedonia. He was killed in battle in 1854 at Spilio, a village in that district. (*EDT* I, 257-258.)

Song 31. Ἡ Ποταμιά / *At the River*
(XIII, 4. Original tonics: *c#′* and *b*.)
Singer: Ioannis Roudas (50).
Variants: *EDT* I, 416; *EDT* III, 137-138; Fauriel, 227-228; Passow, 391; Politis, 164-165.
Mr. Roudas broke off the text in the middle of the fourth strophe and finished out the tune in "nonsense syllables." Because the song is one of the most expressive in the Greek folk literature, I have translated here the variant that appears in Politis. Fauriel (228) points out that the milk of a male rabbit, a famous folk remedy, is symbolic of something that is difficult to obtain.

> A blonde girl was singing on the Trikhas bridge
> piercing songs, full of grief.
> And from her mournful sound, her grievous song,
> the bridge cracked, the river stopped,
> 5 and the spirit of the river jumped out onto the bank.
> A traveler called out from the far ridge:
> "Change the tune, *kori*, sing a different song

so the river can run again and the bridge be put together again,
so the spirit of the river can return to his place."
10 "How can I change the tune, how can I hush my song?
This song I'm singing is a lament
because there's no cure for the pain in my heart.
I lost my mother and my father and nine soldier brothers,
and my beloved was sick in bed
15 and he sent me searching for a cure that was nowhere in this world:
rabbit's cheese and wild goat's milk.
And, by the time I had gone up into the wild mountains and down
to the plains
to hunt the rabbit, to catch the wild goat,
to build a marble *mandra* to make the cheese,
20 my beloved got married to another woman:
he took a rock for his mother-in-law and the black earth for his
wife."

MACEDONIA

PALATIANO is a small village in the district of Kilkis in central Macedonia, about "two days by donkey" from the borders of Yugoslavia and Bulgaria. The Zaralis family, like most of the other families of the village, are shepherds who immigrated there from the Caucasus region of Russia in 1913, when Greece annexed Macedonia after the second Balkan War. The songs were recorded in the Zaralis home on August 16, 1964.

Song 32. ῾Ένας λεβέντης χόρευε / *A "Levendi" Was Dancing*
(XIV, 3. Original tonic: *f*.)
Singer: Nikolaos Tetramidhas (40).
Lines 4-6. See *Songs 17* and *42*.

Song 33. Τά μάγια / *The Bewitching*
(XIV, 10. Sung to the tune of *Song 32*. Original tonic: *f#*.)
Singer: Andreas Zaralis (45).
Variants: *EDT* III, 268-271 (text and music); *IDT*, 324, 374, 508; XV, 3, collected in Thessaly.
Line 5, in the Greek, is short one syllable.

Song 34. Βρύση μου μαλαματένια / *My Gold Fountain*
(XIV, 12. Original tonic: *e*.)
Singer: Andreas Zaralis (45).
Variants: Merlier, 43; X, 9, collected in Epiros.

Song 35. Μιά κοκκινοφορεμένη / *A Girl in a Red Dress*
(XIV, 1. Original tonic: *e´*.)
Singer: Panayiota Zarali (20).
Variant: *IDT*, 508.
The song is probably in 3/4 time. I have transcribed it exactly as Miss Zarali sang it, since she consistently sang the 5/8 bars (i.e., if written in 3/4 time, the third bar of each melodic phrase is shortened). In the following song, sung to the same basic melody, Miss Zarali usually *lengthened*, by an eighth note or more, the third bar of each phrase. A "corrected" version of the melody might be as follows:

Song 36. Σοῦ εἶπα, μάνα, πάνδρεψέ με / *I Told You, Mother, Marry Me Off*
(XIV, 6. Sung to the basic tune of *Song 35*. Original tonic: *f#´*.)
Singer: Panayiota Zarali (20).
Variants: *IDT*, 260-261; Merlier, 34-35; Ricky Holden and Mary Vouras, *Greek Folk Dances*, 103.
In the most common variant of this text the young girl begs her mother not to marry her to an old man, who will be "petty and bothered by small things." (See the variant in Holden and Vouras.)
Lines 7-10. *Kouniadha* and *sinnefadha* both mean "sister-in-law." The first term refers to the husband's sister, and the second to the wife of the husband's brother. The implication in these lines is that the unmarried *kouniadha* will be too busy preparing her dowry, and the *sinnefadha* too busy minding her children, to have any time for the new bride, especially if she falls ill.

Song 37. Ἡ Παναγιωτούλα / *Panayiotoula*
(XIV, 2. Original tonic: *f#´*.)
Singer: Panayiota Zarali (20).
This is a variant of "Ἡ Αἰγιώτισσα" (*Girl of the Aegean*), an island song popular throughout Greece.

KENDRIKON is about an hour's walk from Palatiano. As its name suggests, it is the central town and market place for the surrounding villages. Many of its citizens are Pontic refugees, i.e., people who lived in the Black Sea region of eastern Thrace and who were forced to leave there during the 1923 exchange of populations. The songs, collected from grandchildren of refugees, were recorded in the social hall on August 15, 1964.

Song 38. Κάλαντα τοῦ Λαζάρου / *"Kalanda" for Lazarus Day*
(XXII, 8. Original tonic: c#'.)
Singer: Khristos Liaretidhis (8).

Song 39. Κάλαντα τῶν βαϊῶν / *"Kalanda" for Palm Sunday*
(XXII, 9. Original tonic: c.)
Singer: Miron Ioannidhis (16).

KOUDHOUNIA is a farming village set on a flat dusty plain just outside the market town of Dhrama in central Macedonia. The songs were recorded in the Kamboulidhi home on August 18, 1964.

Song 40. Κάλαντα τῶν Χριστουγέννων / *"Kalanda" for Christmas*
(XXII, 33. Original tonic: c#'.)
Singers: Irini Kamboulidhi (10) and Theodhorea Yiorghadhou (10).
Variants: *EDT* III, 158-159; Passow, 217 (lines 1-4); XXII, 16, collected in Epiros.
Lines 1-4. See *Song 66.*
Line 8. See *Song 43* (line 8) and *Song 109* (line 13).

Song 41. Κάλαντα τοῦ Λαζάρου / *"Kalanda" for Lazarus Day*
(XXII, 32. Original tonic: e'.)
Singers: Irini Kamboulidhi (10) and Theodhorea Yiorghadhou (10).
In many parts of Greece the children act out the death and resurrection of Lazarus while they sing the *kalanda*. (See Megas, 88.) My informants for this *kalanda* sang it as a narrative and a dialogue; i.e., lines 1-2 were sung in unison, lines 3-4 by one singer, lines 5-10 by the other singer, and lines 11-14 in unison again.
Lines 3-10. Compare the dialogue in *Song 91.*

AVLI is a modern village on the main highway outside Kavala. The old Avli is about an hour or so up the mountain behind the village, but only a few families remain there, since the new village is closer to the tobacco fields where the villagers earn their living. The songs were recorded in the informant's home on August 19, 1964.

Song 42. Τραγοῦδι τοῦ γάμου / *Wedding Song*
(XIV, 17. Original tonic: b.)

Singer: Kiriaki Vlakhopoulou (50).
Lines 3-5. See *Songs 17* and *32*.
Lines 7-8 are a separate distich tacked on to the song. When she sang them, Mrs. Vlakhopoulou distorted the tune considerably: she dropped a syllable in line 7 and added "μέ τού γαμπρό" to line 8 instead of following the repetition pattern of the rest of the song.

Song 43. Κάλαντα τῆς Πρωτοχρονιᾶς / "*Kalanda*" *for New Year's*
(XXII, 35. Original tonic: *e* '.)
Singer: Kiriaki Vlakhopoulou (50).
Line 1. A common opening for the New Year's *kalanda* (See *Song 109*).
Lines 2-6. This is a much reduced version of the encounter between Christ and Saint Vasili (see Introduction). It is more complete in *Song 92* (lines 3-12) and *Song 110* (lines 15-23).
Lines 8-10. See *Song 109* (lines 12-15).
Lines 8-14. See Politis, 193.
Lines 16-20. See *Song 92* (lines 24-27).

PANAYIA, a mountain village on the island of Thasos, is distinguished by plane trees, large wooden houses, and water rushing through stone culverts built into the streets. The songs were recorded in the social hall on August 23, 1964.

Song 44. Ἡ Προσφυγούλα / *Prosfighoula*
(XIV, 28. Original tonic: *f#*.)
Singer: Eleni Titiyianni (40).
Line 1. The name Prosfighoula is derived from πρόσφυγας ("refugee").

Song 45. Θέλω νά πάω στήν Ἀραπιά / *I want to go to Arapia*
(XIV, 26. Original tonic: *e♭* '.)
Singer: Eleni Titiyianni (40).
Variants: Pakhtikos, 172; Passow, 409.
Line 1. In colloquial Greek, an *arapis* (dim. *arapaki*) is a black man; it is also used like "bogyman." J.C. Lawson, in *Modern Greek Folklore and Ancient Greek Religion*, 276-277, associates the term with a type of water genie. R.M. Dawkins, in *Modern Greek in Asia Minor*, 227, defines *arapis* as a black giant. See also G.A. Megas, *Folktales of Greece*, lv-lvi and 253 for the *arapis* in folktales. Arapia is not Arabia (which is *Aravia* in Greek), but the "land of the *arapis*."

Song 46. Χελιδόνισμα / *Khelidhonisma*
(XIV, 22. Original tonic: *e* '. The song ends with section A.)
Singer: Eleni Titiyianni (40).

Variant: Passow, 225-226.

The *khelidhonisma*, or "swallow song," is sung as part of the "Procession of the Swallow" when children carry a basket of ivy and a wooden swallow from house to house on March 1st. (See Megas, 82-83.)

Mrs. Titiyianni confused lines 5 and 6 of the Greek text (see footnote to Greek text), and I have "corrected" them in the translation. As she sang them they would read:

Nanny goats start to go up into the branches
Flocks start eating branches

LIMENA is the main harbor village of Thasos. Mrs. Tsongou, the grandmother in the home I stayed in, was disturbed that I had done all my collecting in the village of Panayia and had found no one to sing for me in her village. During the whole week I was there she plumbed her memory for *kalanda* she had heard as a child; she finally came up with several garbled verses of the *kalanda* for New Year's and Lazarus Day, plus the following grace, which she said they used to chant before the midnight cutting of the *vasilopitta* (see Megas, 40-41). The recording took place in Mrs. Tsongou's daughter's home on August 23, 1964.

Song 47. Προσκυνή τοῦ τραπεζοῦ τῆς Πρωτοχρονιᾶς / *Table Grace for New Year's Eve*
(XXII, 39. Chanted rapidly on *d'*.)
Singer: Aryiri Koutoupi Tsongou (75).

Mrs. Tsongou omitted line 5 when she recorded the grace and dictated it to me afterward.

SPORADES ISLANDS

The main village of SKYROS covers the side of a small mountain. Mrs. Tsakami lives in a house at the foot of the village. When she sang, she looked away to the farther mountains, and at one point exclaimed that she couldn't sing properly in the valley: "If only I were up on those mountains there . . ." The songs were recorded in her home on July 23, 1964.

Song 48. Τραγοῦδι τοῦ γαμοῦ / *Wedding Song*
(X, 1. Original tonic: *b*.)
Singer: Evfrosini Tsakami (55).

The song is sung by the newlyweds as they walk in procession, following the musicians, to the village square for the reception dance.

Song 49. Τό καπέλικο / *Shepherd's Song*
(X, 3. Original tonic: *a*.)

Singer: Evfrosini Tsakami (55).
This is a "table" song, sung at the wedding banquet in the evening after the ceremony.

Song 50. Τραγοῦδι τοῦ γάμου / *Wedding Song*
(X, 2. Original tonic: *e*.)
Singer: Evfrosini Tsakami (55).
Variant: Passow, 498.
This is another "table" song (see above).

Song 51. Στόν καλέ / *Ston kale*
(X, 4. Original tonic: *b*.)
Singer: Evfrosini Tsakami (55).
This is a dance song, performed at the wedding reception dance. The song has gained popularity in Athens, where it is known as a lullaby. Mrs. Tsakami insisted that it was not a lullaby and that it was sung only at wedding dances. The title, *Ston kale*, is the Skyriote pronunciation of *sto kalo*, a farewell expression, which means roughly "May you go to success."
Line 8. The "foreign gentleman" may be the speaker's father-in-law (or future father-in-law), since "foreigner" (ξένος) can refer to anyone outside the family, especially if he is from another village or region.

Song 52. Τραγοῦδι τῶν Ἀπόκρεων / *Song for Carnival*
(X, 5. Original tonic: *b*.)
Singer: Evfrosini Tsakami (55).
Carnival activities on Skyros traditionally include a mummer's play, with a masked *kaloyeros* dressed in hides with bells tied around his waist (see Megas, 66-67).

Song 53. Τραγοῦδι τῆς Καθαρᾶς Δευτέρας / *Song for Clean Monday*
(X, 6. Original tonic: *b*.)
Singer: Evfrosini Tsakami (55).
The first day of Lent is known as "clean Monday," a term which derives partly from "the housewives' custom of cleaning their pots and pans with hot water mixed with ashes, but mainly from the fact that this day marks the beginning of a spiritual and bodily purification from the sins . . . committed during Carnival" (Megas, 72).

Song 54. Τραγοῦδι τῆς Πρωτομαγιᾶς / *Song for May Day*
(X, 7. Original tonic: *b*.)
Singer: Evfrosini Tsakami (55).
Although the first of May is celebrated as the festival of spring

throughout Greece, it is also the beginning of the month in which magic spells are most effective. (See Megas, 120-121.)

Song 55. Ὁ Αὐλωνιτιάτικος / *Ravine Song*
(X, 8. Original tonic: *b*.)
Singer: Evfrosini Tsakami (55).

When I asked around SKOPELOS for folk singers I was told to look for "that group of *koritsia* who are always dancing around Christ Church square." The ten girls ranged in age from seven to twelve. Their songs (56-60) were recorded (as the girls danced) in the church square on July 28, 1964, with the whole neighborhood gathered to watch (including a two-year-old who hummed along and chimed in on key words— right next to the mike). The songs are all sung in a leader-response form and end with the following *yirisma* (occasionally leaving out bars 7-8):

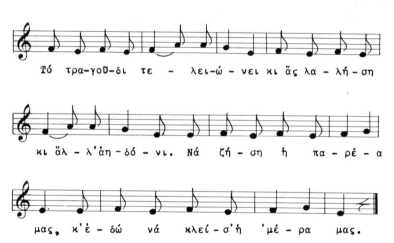

Τό τρα-γοῦ-δι τε - λει-ώ - νει κι ἄς λα - λή - ση κι ἄλ - λ'ἀη - δό - νι. Νά ζή - ση ἡ πα - ρέ - α μας, κ'ἐ - δώ νά κλεί - σ'ἡ 'μέ - ρα μας.

The song is ended
Let another nightingale sing,
And a stone-swallow.

After the last song the girls sang this variant:

Τό τρα-γοῦ-δι τε - λει-ώ - νει κι ἄς λα - λή - ση

κι ἄλ - λ'ἀη-δό - νι   κ'ἔ-να   πε - τρα-χε   -   λι - δό - νι.

The song is ended;
Let another nightingale sing
Long live our company [of friends]
And here ends our day.

The second set of songs (61-66), recorded by members of the Vlakhakis family (Mrs. Karangiozou is Mr. Vlakhakis' sister), also uses the leader-response form. The members of the Vlakhakis family were strikingly individualistic in their singing, and each of the singers, completely sure of his or her own version of the melody and rhythm, sang out without regard for the other voices. The effect was quasi-polyphonic, with the different melodic variants crossing and recrossing one another. The songs were recorded in the Vlakhakis home on July 29, 1964.

Song 56. Στήν ̓Αγιά Παρασκευή / At the Chapel of St. Paraskevi
(IX, 5. Original tonic: *d ́-f# ́.*)
Singers: Paraskevi Sofokitou (12) with chorus of girls.
Variants: *EDT* III, 252; Pakhtikos, 138-139, 167-168.

Song 57. ̔Η ὀρφανή / The Orphan
(IX, 3. Original tonic: *f# ́-g# ́.*)
Singers: Paraskevi Sofokitou with chorus of girls.
Variants: Periklis Khristoforidhis, ̔Ελλάδα, τά τραγούδια τοῦ λαοῦ μας, 6-7; Alexis Poulianos, Λαϊκά τραγούδια τῆς ̓Ικαρίας, 159-163.
In both the above variants, collected in Rhodes and Ikaria, respectively, the ballad continues with the familiar folk tale Cinderella (̔Η Σταχτοπούτα). The dead mother is helped by nature to dress her daughter for the king's ball:

The sun gave her beauty, the morning star charm,
the moon gave her his proud bearing,
the dawn gave her freshness, the fields a skirt,
and the Pleiades diamond stars for a crown.

(Poulianos, 162)

Lines 4-5, 6-7, 11-12, and *13-14* are rhymed couplets; *Lines 7, 9, 12,* and *14* were sung, without repetitions and *tsakismata*, to bars 9-12 of the music.

Song 58. Μπαίνω σ' ἄδειο περιβόλι / I Go into an Empty Orchard

(IX, 2. Original tonic: e ♭ ′-g♯ ′.)
Singers: Stamatia Kalimani (10) with chorus of girls.
Variants: G. Kazavis, Νισύρου Λαογραφικά, 58; the orchard is usually a "wild" (ἄγριο) orchard instead of an empty one (*cf.* Baud-Bovy II, 40). Megas, in Ἑλληνικαί ἑορταί καί ἔθιμα τῆς λαϊκῆς λατρείας, 177, gives this song as an example of the *rousalia*, the carols that are sung from house to house on "white" Saturday or Sunday, i.e., the Saturday or Sunday following Easter. (See Megas, 111.)

Song 59. Στόν ᾿ Ἅδη θά κατέβω / *I'm Going down to Hades*
(IX, 4. Original tonic: f♯ ′-f ′.)
Singers: Stamatia Kalimani (10) with chorus of girls.
Variants: Merlier, 67; XVII, 19, collected in the Peloponnesos.

Song 60. Κυνηγός πού κυνηγοῦσε / *The Hunter Was Hunting*
(IX, 1. Original tonic: f♯ ′-a ′.)
Singers: Katina Vlakhaki (11) with chorus of girls.
This song was originally published (transcribed in a different key and with a different translation) in the *Juilliard Repertory Library*.

Song 61. ᾿ Ἕνας μεγάλος βασιλεᾶς / *A Great King*
(IX, 10. Original tonic: e ′.)
Singers: Mikhail Vlakhakis (45) with members of the Vlakhakis family.
Variant: Poulianos, Λαϊκά τραγούδια τῆς ᾿ Ικαρίας, 85-89.
The rhythm transcribed is inexact. When the chorus of girls that sang the previous songs danced this tune (with a different text), the meter was 17/8: (2+2)+(2+2)+(2+3)+(2+2). Mr. Vlakhakis, however, sang it with beats lengthened at random (and seldom extended to as much as twice the basic value of an eighth note). I have transcribed the song in 2/4 and indicated the lengthened notes in the transcribed (second) strophe, but these are by no means followed throughout.
The ballad is a version of the widespread folk theme of the young woman who dresses up like a man and goes off to war. In Poulianos' Ikarian variant, the tale is more complete, with an extended description of the tasks the young king sets to determine the sex of the strange captain.

Song 62. Μάνα μ᾿, στό περιβόλι μας / *Mother, in Our Orchard*
(IX, 7. Original tonic: c♯ ′.)
Singers: Keretsoula Karangiozou (40) with members of the Vlakhakis family.
Variant: *IDT*, 329.
The musical form should be AABB; however, the chorus was often

slow on the pick-up, and so Mrs. Karangiozou omitted all of the repeats
of the B section and those of the A section in strophes 3-7.

Song 63. Ὁ λειβάδι εἶναι ἀνθισμένο / *The Valley's All in Blossom*
(IX, 13. Sung to the tune of *Song 60*. Original tonic: *e'*.)
Singers: Keretsoula Karangiozou (40) with members of the Vlakhakis
family.

Mrs. Karangiozou tended to distort the meter of whatever she sang,
adding a beat here, half a beat there, and a whole bar somewhere else.
The tune is skeletally the same as the tune for *Song 60*, although both
the rhythmic and the melodic variations make it sound quite different.
The song ended with the following *yirisma*:

Τοῦ-τη γῆ πο'τήν πα - τοῦ-με, Ν-δ-λοι μέ-σα θέ νά μποῦ-με.

This earth we walk on,
we'll all go inside it.

Song 64. Πάλι θ' ἀρχίσω γιά νά πῶ / *Once More Let Me Begin to Tell*
(IX, 12. Original tonic: *e'*.)
Singers: Keretsoula Karangiozou (40) with members of the Vlakhakis
family.

Bars 10-13 are a variant of bars 14-17; in other strophes Mrs. Kara-
giozou sang them closer to the original.

Song 65. Κάτω στόν ἄσπρο ποταμό / *Down by the White River*
(IX, 8. Sung to the tune of *Song 64*. Original tonic: *c#'*. M.m. = 152.)
Singer: Keretsoula Karangiozou (40).
The entire song was sung without repeats.

Song 66. Κάλαντα τῶν Χριστουγέννων / *"Kalanda" for Christmas*
(XXII, 28. Original tonic: *b♭*.)
Singers: Keretsoula Karangiozou (40) with members of the Vlakhakis
family.

Variant: XXII, 26, collected on the island of Paros.
Lines 1-4. See Passow, 217, and *Song 40*.
The missing line (between lines 10 and 11),

'Ολίγο ΰπνο πάρετε καί πάλι σηκωϑῆτε

Go to sleep for a little while and then get up again

clarifies the sequence of events—the *kalanda* are usually sung on Christmas Eve, and the Christmas Day religious service begins at 5:00 A.M.

CRETE

LASITHI is the easternmost province of Crete. Adhamandia Sindikhaki, whose home is in a village outside the provincial capital of Aghios Nikolaos, was a schoolteacher in the tiny village of Vari on the island of Syros. The songs were recorded in the village schoolhouse in Vari on July 24, 1964.

Song 67. Πότε ϑά κάνε ξαστεριά / *When Will the Skies Clear?*
(VIII, 7. Original tonic: *e '*.)
Singer: Adhamandia Sindikhaki (25).
Variant: EDT I, 273; an English translation of another variant appears in Hilary Pym, *Songs of Greece*, 70.
Line 2. Patrona (literally "patroness") is a cartridge box according to J.A. Notopoulos (quoted in *EDT* I, 273). D.A. Petropoulos (*EDT* I, 273) suggests that it may be a personal name for a weapon.
Line 3. Omalo is a plateau on the western edge of the Lefkos mountains in western Crete; Mousouros is the name of a noble family that was established in Crete from the twelfth century (*EDT* I, 273).

Song 68. Τραγοῦδι τοῦ γάμου / *Wedding Song*
(VIII, 8. Original tonic: *e ♭ '*.)
Singer. Adhamandia Sindikhaki (25).
Line 2: A metaphor for the bride and groom often found in wedding songs. (See Chianis, *Folk Songs of Mantineia, Greece*, 102-103; and *IDT*, 482, 483.)
Lines 5-6: In the Greek Orthodox marriage ceremony, the bride and groom are crowned with wreaths made of blossoms and joined together with long streamers. The wreaths symbolize the bonds of marriage; they are kept with the family icons and are often used to swear an oath on. In former times, emperors and other wealthy or important people had wedding wreaths made of gold. Thus, the wish in line 6 is that the bride's children may become wealthy enough to have gold wedding wreaths. (I am indebted to Mary Vouras for this interpretation.)

SITIA is a port in eastern Crete. Yiannis Dhermitzakis, who runs a notions store there, is one of Crete's most famous musicians. He has cut many records for RCA and has published a book of his *mandinadhes*. He proudly displays citations from Kazantzakis, Baud-Bovy, and other notables. He is a virtuoso on both the *lyra* (see below) and the violin, and his skill at extemporizing *mandinadhes* is extraordinary. To demonstrate to me this latter talent he put together the following couplets without any of the usual pauses and part-line repetitions that other singers use in order to give themselves time to put together these formulaic distiches:

'Ο ἄνδρας σας εἶναι καλός, τόπα κι ἐφώναξά το·
ἔχει μουστάκι ὄμορφο καί στό πιγούνι λάσο.

Μιάν ἡ εὐχή πού δίδωσα, γλυκολαλή μου κόρη:
τοῦ χρόνου νἄρθω νά σᾶς δῶ καί νἄχετ᾽ ἕνα ἀγόρι.

Your husband's a good man, I've said it and I've shouted it—
he's got a handsome mustache and a dimple on his chin.

I've got one wish, my sweet-voiced *kori*:
may I come to see you next year and may you have a son.

The songs were recorded in the Dhermitzakis store on July 19, 1967.

Song 69. Μαντινάδες / Mandinadhes
(II, 14. Original tonics: *e* [voice] and *e'* [*lyra*].)
Singer: Yiannis Dhermitzakis (45), *lyra*; accompanied by Dhermitzakis, Jr., on guitar.

The Cretan *lyra* is a small (approximately 18"-22"), three-stringed instrument that is played with a bow. It rests neck-upward on the musician's knee. The strings are tuned a fifth apart and are stopped by the fingernails touching the strings from the side. (See *Instruments*, 38-41.)
In addition to the *lyra* line transcribed here, there is a rhythmic *ostinato*

which Dhermitzakis makes by shaking the bells on his bow as he plays; there is also a kind of drone effect sounded on the open lower two strings (when they are not being used for the melody).

Line 4. I was unable to transcribe the second half of this line. It sounds like "θέρω γιά τήν καρδιά σου" ("I burn for your heart"), which makes no sense in the context. If this is indeed what was sung, it demonstrates what happens when a *mandinadhes* singer is unable to complete his idea—he fills in with a stock formula that will rhyme with his first line.

Song 70. Μαντινάδες / *Mandinadhes*
(II, 3. Original tonics: *g* [voice] and *g'* [violin].)
Singer: Yiannis Dhermitzakis (45), violin.

These distiches, with minor variations, appear in Dhermitzakis' book, Κρητικές Μαντινάδες, 144, 148, 149, 158.

Song 71. Μαντινάδες / *Mandinadhes*
(II, 3. Original tonics: *a* [voice] and *a'* [violin].)
Singer: Yiannis Dhermitzakis (45), violin.

Dhermitzakis went into this tune directly from the preceding one. The distiches are in his book, 27.

DODECANESE ISLANDS

The city of RHODES is divided into two parts: the medieval walled city; and the new city, in which narrow foot streets coexist with wide avenues lined with palms and high-rise hotels. Both the singers, who are sisters, live in the narrow-footstreet quarter. The songs were recorded in Mrs. Savana's home on May 17, 1964.

Song 72. Κάτω χορός / *"Kato" Dance*
(IV, 9. Original tonic: *g'*.)
Singer: Dina Savana (30).
Variant: Baud-Bovy I, 177-182 (melody only).

A *kato* dance is sung and danced when the newlyweds leave the church (Baud-Bovy I, 4).

Line 4. Mrs. Savana actually sang "the angel" instead of "your husband's name." (See Poulianos, Λαϊκά Τραγούδια τῆς Ἰκαρίας, 199.)

Song 73. Τέσσαρα φύλλα ἔχει ἡ καρδιά, Μαρίτσα μου / *The Heart's Got Four Leaves, Maritsa*
(IV, 3. Original tonic: *c'*.)
Singer: Dina Savana (30).

Song 74. Σάν πάῃς, κόρη, στό νερό / *When You Go to the Watering Place*

(IV, 2. Original tonic: *c'*.)
Singer: Dina Savana (30).

Song 75. Καντάδα / *Kandadha*
(IV, 12. Original tonic: *c#'*.)
Singer: Khrysa Saridhou (35).
Line 8. Mrs. Saridhou sang "βοτάνι" instead of "ποτάμι" on the repeat, making the line read "To find the *herb* of forgetfulness, to drink and forget you."

NISYROS is a small island between Rhodes and Kos. Mrs. Laklaridhou, although she had been living in Rhodes for nearly twenty years, still considered Nisyros her real home. The songs were recorded in the Savana home in Rhodes on May 17, 1964.

Song 76. Τό περιβόλι / *The Orchard*
(IV, 10. Original tonics: *b* and *e*.)
Singer: Maria Laklaridhou (55).
Variants: Baud-Bovy II, 195-205; Kazavis, Νισύρου Λαογραφικά, 131-133.
The song is sung on Monday afternoon (after the Sunday wedding) by two choruses of women (Baud-Bovy II, 195).
Lines 1, 2, and *3; 4-5;* and *9-10* are rhymed.
Line 3. Khazimanoli is the name of the bride's father and thus will change according to the family involved.

Song 77. 'Άϋτε, πάρε Φραντζῆ / *Get Your "Lyra," Frandzi*
(IV,11. Original tonic: *b♭*.)
Singer: Maria Laklaridhou (55).
Variant: Baud-Bovy II, 188-189.
Sung the evening of the wedding.
Lines 2 and *4* are sung without the repetition indicated in the B section of the music.

ANDIMAKHIA is a small village set inland on a barren plateau on the island of Kos. I went there looking for a violinist I had heard about, but I arrived just as he was jumping onto the back of a pick-up truck headed for a wedding in another village. "I'll be back in three days, I'll sing for you then"; but I knew that three days of singing and playing would leave him with little voice. (When he returned he whispered his apologies.) The other villagers were distressed at the thought of my going away empty-handed, so various children were dispatched in several directions to find singers. I ended up recording (on May 24, 1964) in the local coffee-house, with thirty or forty people crowded into the small room listening.

Song 78. Τ ῶρα τά πουλιά / *Now the Birds are Singing*
(IV, 8. Original tonic: *b*.)
Singer: Yiannis Sinesios (35).
Variants: Baud-Bovy II, 46-47 (text and music); *EDT* III, 5-6 (text and music).

This is one of the texts associated with Digenes Akrites, hero of the Byzantine oral epic (see John Mavrogordato, ed., *Digenes Akrites*). The dawn is the dawn after a battle in which Digenes had "killed a thousand and wounded a thousand" (from another variant of the text, see *EDT* III, 4-5). The text is now sung, to various tunes, throughout Greece as a wedding song, often at dawn on the morning of the wedding.

Song 79. Τραγοῦδι τῆς νύφης / *Bride's Song*
(IV, 10. Original tonic: *e*′.)
Singer: Yiannis Sinesios (35).

Song 80. Τραγοῦδι τοῦ γάμου / *Wedding Song*
(IV, 21. Original tonic: *e*′.)
Singer: Yiannis Sinesios (35).
The song is sung when the groom goes to the bride's house to inspect the dowry.

Song 81. Τραγοῦδι ποὺ ξυρίσεται ὁ γαμπρός / *Song for Shaving the Groom*
(IV, 22. Original tonic: *d*′.)
Singer: Yiannis Sinesios (35).
Variant: *EDT* III, 285-286 (second strophe and music).
The song is sung while the groom is ceremoniously shaved by the *koumbaros* (best man) just before the procession leaves for the church.

Song 82. Σὰν πᾶς στὰ ξένα, ἀγάπε μου / *When You Go off to the Foreign Lands*
(IV, 13. Original tonics: *e* and *a*.)
Singer: Yioryios Petros (25).
Compare section A of the music and lines 1-2 to the *yirisma* of *Song 9.* *Lines 9-10* are sung to section A of the music.

Song 83. Ἡ Ἐλένη / *Eleni*
(IV, 15. Original tonic: *e* ♭ ′.)
Singer: Nikolaos Avghoulas (60).
The main distich is lines 1 and 4. Lines 2-3 and 5-6 are textually *yirismata*; I have not separated them, because the music to which they are sung is, I feel, an integral part of the tune.

Song 84. Δέν βρίσκεται πονόμετρο / *There's No Pain Meter*
(IV, 20. Original tonic: *e '.*)
Singer: Panayiotis Kandonios (55).

Song 85. Τό ἔρι / *Eri*
(IV, 17. Original tonic: *e '.*)
Singer:Yiannis Sinesios (35).
Both lines of the second strophe are sung to section B of the music.

Song 86. Σάν τό σβυσμένο κάρβουνο / *Like the Burnt-Out Coal*
(IV, 14. Original tonic: *d '.*)
Singer: Yioryios Petros (25).
In the Greek text, the portion of *line 2* in parentheses is extra; it is sung to the music marked between the two asterisks. A similar repetition is not in the second strophe.
Line 3. Literally, "The troubles of this world, I play with them as with *koumboloyi* beads."

Song 87. Δυοσμαράκι / *Little Mint*
(IV, 16. Original tonic: *c '.*)
Singer: Yioryios Petros (25).
Variant: *EDT* III, 248-249 (*tsakismata* and music).
Line 2 is confused in the Greek text (see footnote to Greek text). I am indebted to Professor G.K. Spyridakis for suggesting this solution.

The main port of KALYMNOS is one of the most colorful towns I visited: yellow churches with blue domes, blue houses with white trim, yellow streets, green steps—all bright and freshly painted.

The Bairambis family, a family of shepherds, lived in a house hanging over the water on the edge of town. We recorded in a large room in their home, which was soon filled with the curious, drawn in by the sound of the bagpipe; outside there was impromptu dancing in the street. The session took place on June 2, 1964.

Song 88. Ὁ βοσκός κι ὁ βασιλιᾶς / *The Shepherd and the King*
(V, 11. Original tonic: *e ♭ '* [voice] and *e ♭ "* [bagpipe] .)
Singer: Mikhail Bairambis (55), accompanied by his son Manoli Bairambis (25), *tsambouna*.
Variants: Baud-Bovy I, 193-194 (text and music); *EDT* III, 370-371 (text and music).
The island bagpipe, or *tsambouna*, is made of a goat- or kidskin to which is attached a reed or wooden mouthpiece and a pipe, usually made out of a cow's horn. Fitted into the pipe are two reeds of equal length. The left-hand reed has five holes (six notes), and the right-hand reed has either five holes (playing in unison with the other), three holes (match-

ing the four lowest notes of the other), or one hole (matching the two lowest notes). The range is usually *do-la*, the exact pitch depending on the size of the reeds, mouthpiece, and so on. (See Spyros Peristeris, Ό ᾽Ἀσκαυλος (τσαμπούνα) εἰς τὴν νησιωτικὴν Ἑλλάδα, and *Instruments*, 30-33.)

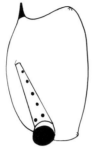

Bairambis' *tsambouna* is of the third type. The range of the left-hand reed is d^b ''-b^b '' ($do=d^b$), and of the right-hand one d^b ''-e^b ''. In the transcription (transposed to *re=d*), the melody of the left hand is represented on the first staff, and the drone of the right-hand reed on the second. The series of high *a*'s also included on the second staff represents a percussive line of sharp squeaks. (I am indebted to Wendy B. Stuart for assistance on this transcription.)

Line 18. Bairambis actually sang "[down] *from* the watering place."

The *tsakisma* of strophe 3 is also used for strophe 6 (lines 11 and 12); all other strophes use the *tsakisma* of strophes 1 and 2.

CYCLADES ISLANDS

SANTORINI (Thira) is the strangely-shaped volcanic island that may have been the original "continent" of Atlantis. Petros Khrysos, whose home is in the main village of Santorini, was a schoolteacher on the island of Syros. His grape-harvesting song was recorded in the schoolhouse in the village of Vari on that island, on July 24, 1964.

Song 89. Τραγούδι τῆς βεντέμας / *Grape-Harvesting Song*
(VIII, 9. Original tonic: *c*.)
Singer: Petros Khrysos (25).

ERMOUPOLIS, the main port on the island of Syros, is the capital of the Cyclades Islands and was, until the latter part of the nineteenth century, Greece's busiest port. The Kondiza sisters ran the small hotel where I stayed; the songs were recorded in the hotel on July 26, 1964.

Song 90. Νανούρισμα / *Lullaby*
(VIII, 14. Original tonic: *b*♭.)

Singer: Evangelia Kondiza (30).
Variants: *EDT* III, 387-388; *IDT*, 433; Politis, 185.

Song 91. Κάλαντα τοῦ Λαζάρου / *"Kalanda" for Lazarus Day*
(XXII, 24. Original tonic: *b* ♭ .)
Singers: Evangelia Kondiza (30) and Marina Kondiza (25).
Variant: *EDT* III, 186-187.

PRODHROMOS, set inland on the island of Paros, is a small, stone village enclosed by a medieval wall. From its perch on the side of a hill, it overlooks the rich farm lands where the villagers earn their living. Penelopi Skiadha, whose family farms tobacco, is the local school-teacher. The *kalanda* was recorded in her home on July 1, 1964.

Song 92. Κάλαντα τῆς Πρωτοχρονιᾶς / *"Kalanda" for New Year's*
(XXII, 25. Original tonic: *b-e* ♭ '.)
Singer: Penelopi Skiadha (25).
Lines 1-2 are a common opening distich for *kalanda* and other types of songs. In Chianis, *Folk Songs of Mantineia, Greece* (131), they begin an engagement song; in John K. Campbell, *Honour, Family, and Patronage* (135), they are part of a Sarakatsanos wedding song.
Lines 3-4. This part of the narrative is usually in the third person; i.e., "He [Christ] went out . . ." See *Song 43* (lines 2-3).
Lines 3-12. See *Song 43* (lines 2-6) and *Song 110* (lines 15-23); also see note to *Song 43*.
Lines 17-21 and *28-30* are part of a "doubled" *kalanda*. See note to *Song 108*.
Line 26. Miss Skiadha actually sang "He's asking for the *white* sheep . . ." but was corrected by her listening family. (See Greek text and footnote.)

CYCLADES ISLANDS
Miss Skiadha broke the *kalanda* at line 20 and again at line 23, each time raising the pitch a whole tone when she started again. The text fits the tune as follows:

Line	Sections of Music Sung to
1	a-b
2-16	c-b
17	c
18	c-b
19	d
20	a
21	a-b

22	c-b
23	a-b
24-27	c-b
28	c
29	c-b
30	d

APIRANTHOS is a large mountain village located in the center of the island of Naxos. The houses, two- and three-story buildings with worked-iron balconies, recall the Venetian influence on the island. I arrived in Apiranthos the day after local elections had taken place, and a large group of men and boys were parading the streets with several folk musicians, singing congratulations to the newly elected officials. *Song 93* below is not the one they were singing that morning, but one from a previous year that Mrs. Zevghola fished out of her memory with the help of a printed version from an old newspaper. *Songs 93* and *94* were recorded in the Zevghola home on July 6, 1964.

The Mandzouranis family, informants for *Songs 95-97*, is also from Apiranthos, but lives in the Khora, where Mr. Mandzouranis is a school-teacher and his son Ioannis is a student at the local *gymnasium*. The songs were recorded in their home in the Khora on July 11, 1964.

Song 93. ᾽Εκλογικό τραγούδι / *Election Song*
(VIII, 19. Original tonic: b ♭.)
Singer: Ekaterini Zevghola (45).
Mrs. Zevghola sang these distiches to about four completely different tunes of which I have transcribed only the first.

Line 9. Protopapadhaki, a former Conservative member of Parliament from Apiranthos.

Line 21. Constantine Karamanlis (b. 1907), former leader of the conservative National Radical Union and prime minister of Greece from 1955 to 1963.

Lines 15 and *22.* Vouli, the name of the House of Parliament in Athens.

Song 94. Κάλαντα τῶν φώτων / *"Kalanda" for Epiphany*
(XXII, 22. Original tonic: b.)
Singer: Konstandinos Kytinis (10).
The song ends at the first double bar line.

Line 4. The singer actually sang ". . . the moon *ray*" instead of "the moon for her breast." (See footnote to Greek text; also Passow, 222.)

Song 95. ᾽Η Βλάχα / *Shepherd Girl*

(VIII, 22. Original tonic: *a*.)
Singers: Kostas Mandzouranis (40), Froso Mandzouranis (35), and Ioannis Mandzouranis (13).

Song 96. Κοτσάκια / *Couplets*
(VIII, 23. Original tonic: *b*.)
Singer: Ioannis Mandzouranis (13).

Song 97. Κοτσάκια ἀντιπολεμικά / *World War II Couplets*
(VIII, 24. Original tonic: *e* ♭ ʹ.)
Singers: Kostas Mandzouranis (40) and Froso Mandzouranis (35).

KATAVATI is a small inland village of the island of Sifnos, a few minutes' walk up the mountain from Apollona, the island's main village. Ioannis Xanthakis, a farmer, and Apostoleos Avranas, a storekeeper, are the musicians for the entire island. The day before our recording session was Saint Marina's day, and the celebration had left their voices hoarse; Samson Loukas, a friend who happened by after the first song, was enlisted to sing the songs as Xanthakis "fed" him the words. The recording was made in the hotel in Apollona on July 18, 1964.

Song 98. Ὁ Φασόλης / *Fasolis*
(VI, 6. Original tonics: *b*♭ [voice] and *b* ♭ ʹ [violin].)
Singer: Samson Loukas (30), accompanied by Ioannis Xanthakis (30), violin, and Apostoleos Avranas (50), *laouto*.

The song appears in Ant. Troullos, Τά λαϊκά χορευτικά τραγούδια τῆς Σίφνου, 7-8. Troullos writes that Fasolis was a real person from the village of Katavati who owned land and flocks of sheep and goats on Khondhropou Mountain in the western part of the island. Like most Greek farmers, he lived in the village and went out each day to tend to his animals; during good weather he spent nights in a small hut on his property, several hours from the village. The ballad apparently recalls a time when he got marooned in bad weather and his loyal apprentice set off to rescue him.

KARDHIANI is a tiny village about an hour by bus from the main port of Tinos. The village consists of one narrow foot street on the side of a mountain overlooking the sea. The whitewashed houses are built above and below the street, which is connected to the main road by stairs. Kostas Panorios was born on the island of Sifnos but has lived in Kardhiani since his marriage and considers it his home. He owns one of the village's three grocery stores, and his two sons, Yiannis and Petros, work the family fields. Panorios is known throughout that part of the island both as a musician and as a storyteller. He has taught his sons the traditional songs, although they both like and play *bouzouki* and western European music as well. The songs were recorded in the Panorios home on July 6, 1967.

Song 99. Μπάλλος σούστα / *"Ballos sousta" Dance*
(VII, 1. Original tonic: *g* [voice] and *g* ' [violin].)
Singer: Kostas Panorios (50), violin; accompanied by Yiannis Panorios (25), *laouto*, and Petros Panorios (20), guitar.
Variant: VI, 1, collected in Sifnos (first couplet only; the tune is similar, too).

Song 100. Τά μάγια / *The Bewitching*
(VII, 5. Original tonic: *e* [voice] and *e* " [violin].)
Singer: Kostas Panorios (50), violin; accompanied by Yiannis Panorios (25), *laouto*, and Petros Panorios (20), guitar.

Song 101. Θά σπάσω κούπες / *I'll Smash Cups*
(VII, 2. Original tonic: *d* [voice] and *d* " [violin].)
Singer: Kostas Panorios (50), violin; accompanied by Yiannis Panorios (25), *laouto*, and Petros Panorios (20), guitar.

Song 102. Τό μπαρμπουνάκι / *Little Red Mullet*
(VII, 4. Original tonic: *e* [voice] and *e* " [violin].)
Singer: Kostas Panorios (50), violin; accompanied by Yiannis Panorios (25), *laouto*, and Petros Panorios (20), guitar.
Line 1. I was unable to transcribe the first four syllables of this line. I think that "μπαρμπουνάκι μου" is misplaced and should come at the end of the half-line; i.e. (with repetitions), as

... μπαρ-, ... μπαρμπουνάκι μου

The full line (without repetitions) would then be:

[3-syllable epithet] μπαρμπουνάκι μου κι ὁλόχρυσό μου ψάρι

Song 103. Ἡ Σακκούλα / *The Money Pouch*
(VII, 6. Original tonic: *d* [voice] and *d* " [violin].)
Singer: Kostas Panorios (50), violin; accompanied by Yiannis Panorios (25), *laouto*, and Petros Panorios (20), guitar.

Song 104. Μπάλλος μαστίχα / *Mastic Ballos Dance*
(VII, 3. Original tonic: *d* ' [voice] and *d* " [violin].)
Singer: Petros Panorios (20), guitar; accompanied by Kostas Panorios (50), violin, and Yiannis Panorios (25), *laouto*.
Variant: Pakhtikos, 35 (first distich only).

Song 105. Μπάλλος / *"Ballos" Dance*

(VII, 7. Original tonics: *e'* [voice] and *g''* [violin].)

Singer: Petros Panorios (20), guitar; accompanied by Kostas Panorios (50), violin, and Yiannis Panorios (25), *laouto*.

Variant: Pakhtikos, 277-278 (first distich only).

The parallel harmony of the music shows the influence of western popular music. The original tune is probably the violin line.

Line 1. Hagia Sofia (Saint Sophia), the famous cathedral in Constantinople (now a museum) that symbolizes for Greeks their claim to that city.

MYKONOS, probably Greece's most popular island, is thronged with international tourists throughout the summer. During the winter months it is (or was, in 1964) left to the villagers and a few expatriate artists. Dances were held every Sunday night in the *zakharoplastion* (a kind of sweet-and-drink shop), and on other nights a bagpiper might appear in the coffeehouse. (When I revisited the island in 1967 I was told that spontaneous folk music was banned from the village and that folk musicians were allowed to play only in a tourist *taverna*.) Aristodhimos Rambias, a tinsmith, and his cousin Mikhail Rambias, were part of the five-member folk orchestra that played for the Sunday-night dances. Mrs. Kousathana runs a dress shop that has become famous with the influx of tourism and has outlets in several American cities. *Songs 106* and *107* were recorded in the summer home of Mrs. Polymeropoulou on January 24, 1964; *Songs 108-110* were recorded in Mrs. Kousathana's home on January 26, 1964.

Song 106. Τῆς τριανταφυλλιᾶς τά φύλλα / *The Leaves of the Rosebush*
(V, 2. Original tonic: *b*.)

Singers: Aristodhimos Rambias (55), *laouto*, and Mikhail Rambias (35), *sandouri*.

The *sandouri* is a kind of dulcimer with a range of three or four octaves, depending on its size. It is played with two hammers made of wood wrapped with cotton or skin at the ends. Each note is given by three to five strings sounding in unison. (See *Instruments*, 42-43; also diagram, below.)

Variants: VI, 2, collected in Sifnos (first distich only); IX, 14, collected in Skopelos (first two distiches only).
I was unable to transcribe the fourth strophe.

Song 107. ʾ Ἀνω Μερά, καλό χωριό / *Good Village Ano Mera*
(V, 1. Original tonic: *c#ʹ.)*
Singers: Aristodhimos Rambias (55), *laouto*, and Mikhail Rambias
(35), *sandouri*.
Variant: H. Pernot, *Melodies populaires grecques de l' île de Chio*, 46
(tune only).
Lines 1, 3, 5. Ano Mera (Upper Place) is a small inland village on
Mykonos, about an hour by bus from the main port.

Song 108. Κάλαντα τῆς Πρωτοχρονιᾶς / *"Kalanda" for New Year's*
(XXIII, 5. Original tonic: *eʹ.)*
Singer: Vienoula Kousathana (55).
Variants: Passow, 220; XXII, 34, collected in Macedonia.
Lines 1-12. Sometimes preceded by lines 1-2 of the following *kalanda*,
these lines make up the New Year's *kalanda* most commonly found
throughout Greece (see Introduction). It is often sung in a "doubled"
variant in which each half of each line is answered by a rhyming half-line
(often totally irrelevant to the text):

ʾ Ἁγιος Βασιλης ἔρχεται–ἄρχοντες τόν κατέχετε,
ἀπό τήν Καισαρεία–σʾεἰσʾ ἀρχόντισσα κυρία

Saint Vasili is coming—notice him, nobles,
from Caesaria—you are a noble lady.

A complete doubled *kalanda* is in Philip Argenti and H.J. Rose, *The
Folklore of Chios*, 643ff. The favorite tune for this *kalanda* (a variant of
the tune for *Song 92*) is in Susan and Ted Alevisos, *Folk Songs of
Greece*, 62. See *Song 92* (lines 17-21 and 28-30).

Song 109. Κάλαντα τῆς Πρωτοχρονιᾶς / *"Kalanda" for New Year's*
(XXIII, 6. Sung to the tune of *Song 108*. Original tonic: *eʹ.)*
Singer: Vienoula Kousathana (55).
Both this and the following *kalanda* are confused, probably due to the
antiquity of the texts. There is a hiatus between lines 2 and 3; the
missing line(s) should introduce the tree described in lines 3-6. (Compare
the miracle tree that springs up in *Song 92*, lines 14-15.)
Lines 12-19. See *Song 43*, lines 8-14.

Song 110. Κάλαντα τῆς Πρωτοχρονιᾶς / *"Kalanda" for New Year's*
(XXIII, 7. Sung to the tune of *Song 108*. Original tonic: *eʹ.)*
Singer: Vienoula Kousathana (55).

Variant: Th. Vanioti, " Ἡ Μύκονος," <u>Κυκλαδικόν Φῶς</u>, 13, no. 152 (1962): 5-6.

Line 3. It is unclear in the original what "it" refers to.

Lines 15-23. Compare *Song 43*, lines 2-6, and *Song 92*, lines 3-12; also see note to *Song 43*.

GLOSSARY

Glossary

(I have transliterated the Greek alphabet according to the usage in S.A. Sofroniou, *Modern Greek*, pp. 14-15, except for "*ου*" which I have transliterated as "ou" instead of "u." Pronunciation is as follows:

a   as in f*a*ther
e   as in r*e*d
i   as in mach*i*ne
o   as in c*o*ne
ou as in y*ou*th

Consonants are pronounced as in English, with the following exceptions:
gh a soft, guttural *g*, similar to the Spanish fue*g*o.
dh like the *th* in *th*ose.
kh like the *ch* in lo*ch*.
r   a single flip of the tongue, as in Spanish, pe*r*o.

When two vowels appear together, they are pronounced separately, as in n*a*ïve.)

Aféndi (pl. *afendádhes*). Lord, master; also, sir (from Turkish *effendi*).
Arápis (dim. *arapáki*). Familiar for a black person; also used like bogyman. See note to *Song 45*.
Arghendiní. An old Athenian coin, worth ten lepta.
Arkhóndissa. Daughter or wife of an *árkhondas*: formerly a "noble," but now any wealthy person.

Bállos. A couple dance in duple time.

Éri. A euphonic word, without meaning, often used at the beginning of a line.

Grósi (pl. *grósia* or *grosa*). A piastre, a Turkish coin used in Greece during the Turkish Occupation.

Kálanda. A carol sung at Christmas, New Year's, Epiphany, Lazarus Day, and Palm Sunday.
Kalóyeros. Literally "monk." One of the protagonists of the mummer's plays performed at Carnival in different parts of Greece.
Kamára. A woman or girl who has a proud bearing or in whom one can take pride.

Kandádha. A modern type of folk song.

Káto dance. A slow dance in duple time that is performed after the wedding ceremony.

Kaiménos. Poor, unfortunate, or one who is misfortunate.

Khelidhónisma. A "swallow" song or song for March 1st (see note to *Song 46*).

Kléft. A mountain guerrilla of the Revolutionary War period and after (see fn. 4 to Introduction).

Kóri. A girl or young woman.

Koumbolóyi. A secular rosary carried by Greek men.

Kouloúri (pl. *koulouria*). A small ring-shaped biscuit.

Kouniádha. Sister-in-law, i.e., the sister of the husband or the wife.

Laoúto. A four-stringed fretted instrument.

Leftá. Small change.

Levéndi. A brave and handsome young man.

Loukoúmi. Turkish delight.

Lýra. A small three-stringed bowed instrument. See note to *Song 69*.

Mána. Mother.

Mandinádhes. Rhymed distiches in the fifteen-syllable iambic meter.

Mándra, mandrí. A fold or pen for animals.

Manoúla. Diminutive of *mana*, used affectionately.

Monógrosi (pl. *monógrosia, monógrosa*). See *grósi*.

Pallikári (pl. *pallikária*). Formerly a member of a *kleft* band; now any young man.

Patróna. Literally "patroness," but in Crete an ammunition box. (See note to *Song 67*.)

Pedhí (pl. *pedhiá*). Literally "child." Used as a term of address.

Pénema (pl. *penémata*). Praise. See Introduction.

Polítikos. Of or from Constantinople (*i Poli* = the City).

Ston kalé (=*sto kaló*). A farewell, literally "go to success."

Sinnefádha. Sister-in-law, i.e., the wife of the brother-in-law.

Syrtós. A circle dance in duple time.

Táliro (pl. *tálira*). A five-drachma coin.

Tamboúra. A hand drum.

Tsákisma (pl. *tsakísmata*). A word or phrase interjected into the line of a song.

Tsámikos. A circle dance in 6/4 meter.

Vilayets (*vilaétia*). Administrative districts (from the period of the Turkish Occupation).

Yiá sou. Literally "Your health." Used as a greeting, a toast, etc.

Yírisma. (pl. *yirísmata*). A couplet sung at the end (or sometimes in between strophes) of a song.

REFERENCES

References

(Comprehensive bibliographies of Greek folk music are found in *Grove's Dictionary of Music and Musicians*, III, 275-277 [New York: Macmillan, 1955]; and Jaap Kunst's *Supplement to the Third Edition of Ethnomusicology* [The Hague: Nijhoff, 1960].)

Abbott, G.F. *Macedonian Folklore*. Cambridge: Cambridge University Press, 1903.

Alevisos, Susan, and Ted Alevisos. *Folk Songs of Greece*. New York: Oak Publications, 1968.

Argenti, Philip, and H.J. Rose, *The Folklore of Chios*, vol. II. Cambridge: Cambridge University Press, 1949.

Baggally, J.W. *Greek Historical Folksongs: The Klephtic Ballads in Relation to Greek History (1715-1821)*. Chicago: Argonaut Inc., 1968. (Reprint of original edition, Oxford, 1936.)

Baud-Bovy, S. *Etude sur la chanson cleftique avec 17 chansons cleftiques de Roumélie transcrites d'après les disques des Archives Musicales de Folklore*. Athens: Collection de l'Institute Francais d' Athènes, 1958.

——. Τραγούδια τῶν Δωδεκανήσων. 2 vols. Athens: I.N. Sidheris, 1935 and 1938.

Campbell, John K. *Honour, Family, and Patronage: A Study of Institutions and Moral Values in a Greek Mountain Community*. London: Oxford University Press, 1964.

Chianis, Sotirios. *Folk Songs of Mantineia, Greece*. Berkeley and Los Angeles: University of California Press, 1965.

——. "Some Observations on the Mixed-Dance in the Peloponnesus." Λαογραφία, 18 (1959): 244-256.

Dawkins, R.M. *Modern Greek in Asia Minor*. Cambridge: Cambridge University Press, 1916.

Dhermitzakis, Yiannis. Κρητικές μαντινάδες. Sitia, Crete, 1963.

Fauriel, Claude. Δημοτικὰ τραγούδια τῆς συγχρόνου Ἑλλάδα. Athens: Nikos D. Nikas, 1956. (A one-volume reprint and translation of *Chants populaires de la Grece moderne*, Paris, 1824.)

Friedel, Ernestine. *Vasilika: A Village in Modern Greece*. New York: Holt, Rinehart, and Winston, 1965.

Holden, Ricky, and Mary Vouras. *Greek Folk Dances*. Newark, N.J.: Folkraft, 1965.

Ioannides, C.D. Φωνητικά γυμνάσματα καί παιδαγωγικά τραγούδια. Nicosia, Cyprus: Bureau of Education, 1963.

Julliard Repertory Library. Cincinnati: Canyon Press, 1970.

Kazavis, G. Νισύρου λαογραφικά. New York: Divry, 1940.

Khristoforidhis, Periklis. Ελλάδα, τά τραγούδια τοῦ λαοῦ μας. Athens, n.d.

Lawson, J.C. Modern Greek Folklore and Ancient Greek Religion: A Study in Survivals. Hyde Park, N.Y.: University Books, 1964. (Reprint of original edition, Cambridge, 1910.)

Makriyannis. The Memoirs of General Makriyannis: 1794-1864. Edited and translated by H.A. Lidderdale. London: Oxford University Press, 1966.

Mavrogordato, John, ed. Digenes Akrites. London: Oxford University Press, 1963.

Megas, G.A. Ελληνικαί εορταί καί έθιμα τῆς λαϊκῆς λατρείας. 2nd ed. Athens: Rhodis, 1963.

———. Folktales of Greece. Chicago: University of Chicago Press, 1970.

———. Greek Calendar Customs. Athens: Rhodis, 1963. (A translation of Ελληνικαί..., omitting some of the songs.)

———, and Spyros Peristeris. Folk Music of Greece. New York: Folkways Records and Service Corp., 1955. (Descriptive notes accompanying Ethnic Folkways Library Album P454, recorded by James A. Notopoulos.)

Merlier, Melpo. Τραγούδια τῆς Ρούμελης. Athens: Sidheris, 1931.

Michaelides, Solon. The Neohellenic Folk-Music. Limassol, Cyprus: Nicosia, 1948.

Notopoulos, James A. Modern Greek Heroic Oral Poetry. New York: Folkways Records and Service Corp., 1959. (Notes accompanying Ethnic Folkways Library Album FE 4468, recorded by James A. Notopoulos.)

Pakhtikos, G. 260 δημώδη Ελληνικά άσματα, vol. 1. Athens: P.D. Sakellariou, 1905.

Passow, Arnoldus. Τραγούδια Ρωμάϊκα: Popularia Carmina Graeciae Recentioris. Athens: Nikas and Spanos, 1958. (A facsimile of the original edition, Leipzig, 1860.)

Peristeris, Spyros. Ο ασκαυλος τσαμπούνα εἰς τήν νησιωτικήν Ελλάδα, Athens: Academy of Athens, 1961. (Reprinted from the Επετηρίδες τοῦ Λαογραφικοῦ Αρχείου, vols. 13 and 14 [1960-1961].)

———. Ο εξάσημος ρυθμός εἰς τά Ελληνικά Δημοτικά Τραγούδια. Athens: Academy of Athens, 1964. (Reprinted from the Επετηρίδες τοῦ Λαογραφικοῦ Αρχείου, vols. 15 and 16 [1962-1963].)

Pernot, Hubert. Melodies populaires grecques de l'île de Chio. Paris: Imprimerie Nationale, 1903.

Plomer, William. *Ali the Lion.* London: Jonathan Cape, 1936.

Politis, N. ' Εκλογαί ἀπό τά τραγούδια τοῦ 'Ελληνικοῦ Λαοῦ. 4th ed. Athens: Vayionaki and Ghrighoropoulou, 1958.

Poulianos, Alexis. Λαϊκά τραγούδια τῆς ' Ικαρίας. Athens, 1964.

Pym, Hilary. *Songs of Greece.* London: The Sunday Times, 1968.

Sofroniou, S.A. *Modern Greek.* London: The English Universities Press, 1962.

Spyridakis, G.K. et al. '' Εκθεσες 'Ελληνικῶν λαϊκῶν μουσικῶν ὀργάνων / *Exposition d'Instruments de musique populaires grecs.* Athens: Ministry of Education and Religion, 1965.

Spyridakis, G.K., G.A. Megas, and Dh. Petropoulos. 'Ελληνικά δημοτικά τραγούδια: 'εκλογή, vol. 1. Athens: Academy of Athens, 1962.

Spyridakis, G.K., and Spyros Peristeris. 'Ελληνικά δημοτικά τραγούδια: μουσική 'εκλογή, vol. 3. Athens: Academy of Athens, 1968.

Thumb, Albert. *A Handbook of Modern Greek.* Chicago: Argonaut Inc., 1964.

Troullos, Ant. Τά λαϊκά χορευτικά τραγούδια τῆς Σίφνου. Sifnos, 1960.

Vanioti, Th. " 'Η Μύκονος." Κυκλαδικόν Φῶς, 13, no. 152 (1962): 5-6.

Yiagas, Athanasios Kh. ' Ηπειρωτικά δημοτικά τραγούδια, 1000-1958. Athens: Pyrros, 1959. (Published by the Institute for Epirotic Studies.)

INDEX OF GREEK TITLES
AND FIRST LINES

INDEX OF GREEK TITLES
AND FIRST LINES